THE BURNING EDGE

EDGE

TRAVELS THROUGH IRRADIATED BELARUS

ARTHUR CHICHESTER

INTRODUCTION

I wrote this book about three and a half years ago, long before the idea of starting a YouTube channel ever entered my mind. I had always had this need to do something creative and escape my life on the factory floor even if just once in my life and writing a book it seemed would be the simplest way to do so. Well it wasn't quite as simple as I thought it would be.

The truth is I never expected anybody to actually read it beyond my mom and perhaps one or two friends who might have felt compelled to do so out of some kind of loyalty, or more likely just to have a laugh at my attempt at being a writer. To be honest the idea was as ridiculous to me as it was to them. Well that is exactly what happened for the first few months after its release. Nobody bought or read it and I went back to the factory. However life then took an unexpected turn and I somehow fell into starting a channel on YouTube that for some reason became quite popular which is no doubt how you ended up discovering this book. Life is unpredictable to say the least.

I look back on the journey you're about to read as a reconnaissance trip for the journeys I later took as Bald and Bankrupt, although of course I never realised that at the time. Belarus and in particular the irradiated eastern corner of the country left a deep impression on me during my wanderings there whilst collecting stories for the book, so much so that when I started the channel I knew I had to return and to introduce viewers to some of the characters that call the region home. You will probably recognise some of the locations you are going to read about from some of my films; Bobruisk bus station, my vodka fuelled picnic film was shot next to jolly Vova's house in the Pokats valley, the town of Chechersk where I met Viktor and Robert and some other locations you may spot.

Re-reading the book recently to write this newly added introduction was of course an endeavour in cringe. There is so much I would change and do differently if I wrote it again but I have resisted the temptation to change things too much, just a few small things deleted or added here and there to improve the narrative from the first edition. The one thing that may confuse you is the pseudonym Arthur Chichester. Back when I originally the book I had no desire to ever put my name or face out there into the world in any way. I was and still am a private person to a large extent and so a pseudonym seemed like a good idea. Little did I know that not long after it was published millions of people would see me generally making a fool of myself on camera in locations stretching from India to the badlands of Bolivia. I kept the pseudonym however, merely because once a book is published under a certain name and has been issued an ISBN number the author name cannot be changed.

Well I hope you enjoy the book. In some ways it is the origin story of the channel where I began to travel for the first time in a way I do in my films, by jumping on a bus heading somewhere and seeing what happens. At the very least you will get a deeper insight into this forgotten corner of Europe. And finally, don't worry, there is lots of vodka, babushkas and the occasional Soviet bus stop contained within the pages.

Ben

Moscow

27th March, 2020

Follow your dreams Chigs...but first go and do your homework

DEDICATION

On the edge of a dark wood situated in a northern suburb of the Belarusian capital stands a white church. High in the tower the bearded priest grips the rope with powerful hands and collapses his cloaked body to the ground, sending the reverberating sound of the iron bell out over the treetops where it dissipates into the night sky.

Inside the church and watched over by incense stained icons, a coffin lays on a table surrounded by the friends and family of the middle-aged man it contains. The deceased lies in his best suit with a peaceful contented look on his face as though he's just resting after a long day at work. The women present, all with their heads covered by dark lace, take turns to read prayers from the Orthodox Bible at the lectern, filling the large echoey hall with the gentle sound of ancient Slavonic words I do not understand. Meanwhile us men sit beside the coffin in thoughtful silence, our stares alternating between the face of our recently deceased friend and our own clasped hands. No doubt like myself they are contemplating their own mortality and how a man who had recently seemed so healthy could now be lying here in the wooden box in which he shall soon be buried.

Perched close to the coffin on a small wooden stool is the deceased man's mother, an elderly woman with deep wrinkled features whose face reminds me of all the other elderly babushkas I have seen on my travels through the Eastern Slavic lands. She has not taken her eyes off her dead son's face since I arrived an hour earlier and will end up staying the night beside him, refusing to leave his side and take rest despite others offering to take her place, assuring her that her son shall not be left alone even for a minute. The partner of the dead man, a beautiful red haired woman dressed head to toe in mourning black like all the women in the hall, silently makes tea and sandwiches in the cramped kitchen at the back of the church for the mourners who have come to pay their respects at this late hour of a summer's evening. She masks her pain with smiles and by feigning interest in the small talk at the church's kitchen table; mundane conversations we engage in to somehow cope with the brevity of the situation. But I sense that she isn't really with us. Her mind is no doubt elsewhere, somehow trying to come to terms with the sudden and unexpected loss of her partner and friend, and I expect with what the future holds for her, knowing that whatever it is she will have to face it alone. Just a couple of months before I had been in their apartment sharing a meal at their kitchen table in the suburbs of the city, singing Russian folk songs and toasting their health. And now so suddenly, so unexpectedly, this.

The man in the coffin, holding a small wooden cross in his carpenter's hands, made the bed on which I slept whilst I was in Minsk. It was the bed in which one night I woke and in the darkness lay imagining a journey into the radiated forests of Belarus.

His name was Igor and this book is dedicated to his memory.

PROLOGUE

I write this from a rundown hotel room constructed long ago in a small bleak town hacked out of the dark forests that surround it. It is a place where outsiders rarely visit and where those with the opportunity to do so have left long before.

Outside through the cracked window, as the evening darkness rolls in slowly over the grey concrete I see Lenin watching me. His arm is held aloft pointing somewhere towards the abandoned factories that stand guard on the edge of town, encasing this forgotten corner of Europe inside a wall of cracked cement and rusting rebar. In contrast to the emaciated people who walk the streets in this distant outpost of the country Lenin is well cared for, his plinth freshly painted, the black tiles beneath his thick shoes shiny and new.

At one end of the square the same people whom I have spent the last few weeks travelling among huddle under a bus shelter decorated with old bathroom tiles to avoid an unexpected evening downpour, all waiting for their way out of the town to arrive. To where I don't know. This town situated in what locals collectively call the 'Zone', is surrounded by smaller villages and settlements where life is even harder, where the people feel even more neglected by a government which does not have the means to provide well for them. Places unknown to all but those who live there, but where despite the hardness of a life lived in a land that has suffered the cruelest of fates, the spirit of the Belarusian people refuses to be extinguished.

Belarus is you could say with some justification, a land synonymous with suffering. A historical pawn of greater powers: Poles, French, Swedes and Germans have all rolled over this nation's flat marshy ground by horse's hoof and tank's track, trampling all who resisted beneath them. And when no enemy appeared from the forests to the west they were killed instead by their Slavic brothers from the east in terrors and reforms done in the name of failed ideologies. Nowhere suffered more in the 20th century than this small green land, its soil stained red as though the national flag were turned upside down.

Every town and village I visit possesses a memorial inscribed with the names of men and women who left to fight for their land, for their family, or often not knowing for what exactly, but who none the less never returned. Blood lines that had survived unbroken since distant times destroyed in an instant by bayonet and bullet, the only reminder to their very existence a name scratched in stone. And as though the land and its people had not suffered enough, in 1986 Belarus suffered one final cruel invasion, a victim again through no fault of its own.

When the reactor exploded at Ukraine's Chernobyl nuclear plant on that fateful day in April it sent its deadly poison up into the night sky from where it slowly drifted north over the border before settling down onto the towns, forests, rivers and farmlands of this small country, infecting everything and everyone in some way.

I have spent the last few weeks riding antiquated buses and suburban trains to the end of every bumpy line. Walked muddy roads and remote forest tracks, staying in run down provincial hotels and wooden cottages in ancient villages unmarked on modern maps, a flaneur of the nation's hinterland, wanting to see for myself a corner of Europe so little known to outsiders.

It's now half past nine and the passengers sheltering beneath the bus stop are gone. The town square is empty except for Lenin who stands awake in the darkness. A few lights dimly shine out from the pre-fabricated apartment buildings opposite, and as the rain rattles the window of my hotel room I return to my bed and fall asleep to the voice of a moustached president speaking from the television screen in the corner.

PREFACE

S omehow unexpectedly I had ended up living in Minsk, the austere capital of the Republic of Belarus, studying at the State Linguistic University that is situated just a stone's throw from the eternal flame which commemorates the victory over the Fascists who had burned and slaughtered their way across the country almost eighty years before.

My original plan had been to go to Moscow for my studies but a sudden last minute demand for more tuition money than originally agreed upon had left me hastily searching around for an alternative school on a matter of principle. Phone calls were made to Bakelite telephones and faxes sent to unfamiliar international dialling codes until a week later I found myself waiting for an interview in a small subterranean room at the Belarusian embassy building tucked away in a salubrious corner of West London. An hour later I had my visa and a week after that I landed at Minsk 2, the capital's functionally named international airport.

The Russian language course I had enrolled on would I hoped, take me from the conversational level I had arrived in the country with to somewhere further along the road towards a functional fluency. However not long after the start of my studies it became clear that the rigid classroom environment with its endless grammar drills and stuffy 19th century text translations that my elderly lecturers insisted upon feeding us were not wholly conducive to my improvement. That just wasn't the way I learned. I needed to speak to people.

To alleviate the boredom I would spend much of my lessons looking out of the window gazing at the grey apartments and office buildings opposite, imagining the lives and events going on inside them: office intrigues, spousal affairs, celebrations and crimes hidden behind impenetrable velour curtains...It was there that I decided I would seek to improve my Russian instead.

I had arrived in Belarus determined to suppress any preconceived notions as to what exactly would await me, trying as much as possible to ignore what was written about the country and its infamous 'Last Dictator' as the Western press had labelled the President. To read newspaper articles and books written by academics and journalists was to believe that Belarus was an oppressive state akin to North Korea where the inhabitants lived lives cowering in constant fear, all the while being spied upon by an ever present secret police force that was willing to do away with anyone who dared criticise. Once stamped into the country by the friendly immigration officer however, I soon realised that all that was just a lazy misconception written by people who had a taste for gross exaggeration and books to sell. Despite the warnings I was never followed by men in trench coats, my room wasn't bugged, nor unfortunately was I honey-trapped by beautiful women wanting to compromise me. It was all a bit disappointing, a bit too normal.

The natives were a gregarious and outspoken bunch who possessed an extremely dry humour that made living there a hugely enjoyable experience. Good friendships were formed easily and when classes were over for the day I'd head out to spend my evenings at kitchen tables in apartments located at the end of buckled tram lines in the rougher outer regions of the city such as the down at heel worker's quarter of Serebranka. Places where foreigners such as myself attracted the attention of the local gopniks who stood swigging beer on street corners. And it was there in those Soviet housing estates where along with new found friends I'd sink endless bottles of the locally produced Wild Duck vodka and sing the songs of Tsoi and Vysotsky, all the time gradually improving my Russian to a point to where it was good enough to ask the questions I wanted to ask even if I did not always understand the answers.

The people were keen to discuss politics and current affairs. In supermarket queues, on trams and buses or in apartment kitchens where I spent my evenings, locals gave their opinions about life and politics in Belarus openly. People did not hold back in their criticisms of the Government or the President and what changes they would like to see. Nobody lowered their voice so as to not be overheard or looked over their shoulder before saying what they thought. As one friend scoffed early on during my stay when I asked if people were afraid to speak openly; 'We are the

grandchildren of the men and women who defeated the Nazis.'
The meaning was clear.

Friends occasionally reminisced about growing up in distant
towns and villages located along the Russian border in the east of
the country, and how after Chernobyl they had been forced to
evacuate those very towns and villages they had been raised in,
leaving behind all they had known. What became rapidly clear
was that there were two Belarus'; there was Minsk with its
shopping centres and trendy wine bars and five star hotels and
then there was the hinterland which was an altogether different
place. A place that seemingly came to a standstill when the first
radiation particles began to rain down all those years ago. A place
that few who left seemingly ever had a desire to go back to.

And so despite my Russian steadily improving I was always
acutely aware of the fact that I could only know so much about a
country whilst sat at a kitchen table in the capital. If I wanted to
know Belarus better, and what it was my friends had left behind,
I'd have to go see for myself and venture out beyond the forests
that encircled Minsk.

As my flight took off and I headed back to London at the end
of my studies I looked out of the window of the Russian built
plane and gazed down at a green land sprinkled with small
wooden villages that were seemingly of another time altogether.
Then the plane banked and Belarus disappeared from view
beneath the grey clouds. At that moment I made a promise to
myself that one day I would return

ONE

On a hot summer's morning I left Kiev, the golden domed capital of Ukraine heading north on a melting provincial highway. It was almost three years to the day since I had watched Belarus disappear beneath the clouds. Earlier I had crossed the wide Dnieper river that dissected the city and ridden the metro to the last stop on the east bank, the rundown area of Lisnaya where Kiev's poorest residents (Turkish students and washed up sex tourists) resided in crumbling concrete towers surrounded by the factory workers and locals who despised them. I exited the heavy doors of the metro station and walked along the two lane highway, passing beyond the metal kiosks and roadside prostitutes who stood in the fish-netted uniform of their profession, and there on an empty stretch of the heat buckled road held my hand out looking for a lift north to the border. Soon afterwards a rusting Volkswagen with Belarusian plates pulled up beside me. I climbed in the back, wedging myself in amongst cardboard boxes and plastic shopping bags emblazoned with familiar brand names.

Vitali and Irina, a Belarusian couple in their early thirties, were returning home to Minsk from a shopping trip to the Ukrainian capital where prices for just about everything were substantially lower than back home. My plan to travel through rural Belarus raised barely contained laughs.

'What do you think you are going to see there? The provinces are just full of drunks,' Irina said, not taking her eyes off the pencil straight road that stretched out through the forest ahead of us.

'That's all we have in our towns, drunk men and their suffering women working to keep food on the table. Better go to Nesvizh castle instead, it's very beautiful.'

Once past Kiev's satellite town of Brovary with its skyline of cranes and half built apartment buildings the road towards the border became emptier and the villages through which we passed visibly poorer. Just before the city ancient of Chernigov, with its gilded church roofs, as a summer rain storm exploded over the endless fields of sunflowers, we turned westwards onto a rough road which was deserted except for the occasional old car displaying Belarusian plates.

We were headed to a little used border post that straddled the muddy banks of the Dnieper which flowed down through Russia and Belarus before entering Ukraine on its way towards the Black Sea, hundreds of miles to the south.

As we sped on elderly village residents sat by the side of the road in front of their wooden cottages scratching a living by selling an assortment of home-grown fruit and vegetables on small rickety tables. Poverty was not just limited to the rural regions of Ukraine however. Kiev was now full of pensioners lining up in food queues at charity trucks waiting for a ladle of soup and a chunk of bread. Others had resorted to selling assorted detritus collected over a lifetime on suburban pavements hoping to earn a hryvna or two. There were however few takers for their broken Soviet remnants. Ukraine after Maidan, or as it had been officially named by some think-tank, 'The Revolution of Dignity', was an infinitely harder place to live for most of the population than it had been before Yanukovich had been forced to flee eastwards towards the safe embrace of Russia. Even staunchly pro-Maidan Ukrainian friends of mine were questioning if it had all come at too great a cost. The answer to that question was no doubt written large on the faces of the pensioners that had been reduced to begging in the city's underpasses and the new stolen contours of the nation's borders.

Eventually we came to a forlorn border post which consisted of nothing more than a collection of corrugated huts above which the Ukrainian flag limply fluttered in the afternoon breeze. Surrounded by nothing but forest and far from the nearest town it was a bleak outpost for a border guard to have to while away his career checking the passports of the few travellers who passed by on this rarely used back-route between the two countries.

A young fresh faced guard with rainwater gushing off his cap's wide brim inspected our passports before stamping them firmly and waving us through with a smile and a cheerio. Ukraine may have been reduced to a shell of what it had been but the natural friendliness of the Ukrainian people was as unwavering as ever. We drove up and over a rough concrete bridge which spanned a river that flowed wide and slow beneath us, the colour of cobalt as it meandered between fenceless fields of tall grasses where chestnut horses grazed in the downpour. Vitali weaved the car between concrete bollards until after a kilometre we pulled up at the Belarus custom's post. A platinum blonde border guard in a neatly pressed uniform handed me an immigration card as I entered the hut.

'I've never seen a British passport before,' she cheerily informed me whilst closely inspecting it under a fluorescent light.

It was still possible to feel like a pioneer in this part of the world.

Eventually after making a phone call and repeatedly scanning my passport pages with a quizzical look on her made-up face she squashed the orange rubber entry stamp onto my visa, the command was given to raise the barrier, and on we drove into a land of dark impenetrable forests the type of which inhabit European fairytales.

TWO

On April 28, 1986 radiation detectors at a Swedish nuclear plant began to twitch rapidly as alarms sounded. At first the scientists believed that a nuclear bomb must have been detonated. However, as alarms started to trigger at plants all across Europe and then further afield, the source of the radiation was traced to the little known nuclear power plant of Chernobyl, located in what was then the Ukrainian Soviet Socialist Republic. A few days later and after endless denials, the Soviet government led by Mikhail Gorbachev reluctantly admitted that there had indeed been an accident and millions of deadly radiation particles had been thrust into the Soviet skies.

I remember returning home from school around that time and finding my mother and father glued to a news report which showed grainy images of men covered in lead suits climbing down from helicopters onto a vast destroyed roof and rapidly shovelling debris into a gaping hole of torn steel and concrete from where smoke escaped into the pale blue sky.

In the following weeks teachers at school asked us to fill shoe boxes with anything we could spare: old toys, clothes and books which were then be sent to schools in the region most affected by the disaster, namely what was then the unheard of Soviet Republic of Belarus. We were encouraged to enclose letters addressed to children we would never know nor fully understand exactly what it was that they had suffered. And then not long afterwards, when it was clear that the radiation would not affect us in any life changing way in Britain, the news programmes moved onto other stories and the greatest of man-made disasters was slowly forgotten about.

However, whilst we who lived far from the tragedy returned to our lives and carried on as before, those in the regions directly affected by the Chernobyl accident did anything but. Far away at the other end of the Continent, people north of the reactor who had lived in the path of the falling radiation particles that sunny April morning and the days which followed, were being evacuated from their homes in towns and villages all along the eastern edge of their small Soviet republic. Whilst we in England gathered around our television sets to watch the World Cup that year, in the forests of Belarus, villages were being bulldozed and buried beneath the contaminated soil and hospitals were rapidly filling with the first influx of sick people.

That was over thirty years ago and yet despite the winters and summers that have passed, the people of Belarus continue to suffer

THREE

On winding roads we sped through orderly villages and towns: Komarin, Savichi, Bragin. This was the backwaters of a country that was itself the backwaters of the Continent. When friends back home had asked me where I was preparing to travel my response had usually drawn confused expressions, not sure if they had misheard. Like the nation of Syldavia from the Tin Tin comics, nobody was quite sure if Belarus really existed at all. Eventually I just started replying 'Russia' whenever anyone asked.

Irina continued to point out what she considered to be the folly of my travel plans.

'Look at these places,' she said as we passed through poor wooden villages strung out along the empty rural highway.

'What are you going to see here? Nesvizh has a beautiful castle, tourists usually go there. Let us take you.'

When I insisted that pretty castles and tourist sights held no real interest for me and that I was more interested in seeing

11

something of the hinterland, regardless of the drunks, she changed tack.

'Someone could kill you, people don't have much out here and you're a foreigner. Tell him Vitali.'

But her husband seemed more positive about my trip.

'You will not be killed,' he promised cheerily before adding, 'but you will almost certainly be robbed.'

I knew however that the only inconvenience I might possibly face would be that of the loneliness one occasionally suffers as a solo traveller on the road.

And it was all along that road, on the neat grassy verges on the edge of the dark woods that we sped past, that small signs began appearing at regular intervals. Painted bright red and yellow and depicting a skull above the words 'ENTRY FORBIDDEN', they were the first hints of what had befallen the region.

FOUR

The town we were heading towards stood on the edge of the official Chernobyl Exclusion Zone, a huge tract of the country evacuated and sealed off with guard posts and road barriers from all but the few scientists and forest rangers who worked inside it. It would be hundreds, if not thousands of years before the land within would be safe enough for regular human habitation again. However by looking at the map and tracing the boundary of the official Zone with large towns such as Mozyr and Hoiniki sitting just outside, it was glaringly obvious that it had been created with more than just radiation levels in mind, it had been created as well by simple economics. Certain towns had simply been too big and expensive to evacuate. Either that or by some immense fluke or Godly intervention the majority of Chernobyl's fallout had landed on villages and forest alone and none of the larger towns. In other words, although towns like Hoiniki or Bragin lay just outside the exclusion zone, they were I was willing to bet no less radiated than many of the evacuated villages within it.

13

We eventually turned off the highway at a junction marked with large concrete letters spelling out the name of the town Hoiniki from where my journey into the country would begin. Vitali guided us through the quiet streets of the distant outpost of the country until pulling up outside the town's hotel, a squat Soviet construction set back from the road in a pretty garden of apple trees. I leveraged myself out of the overloaded Volkswagen and offered some money towards the petrol which was refused with a wave of the hand. As the car drove off I could see Irina shaking her head, no doubt she was telling Vitali that I should have gone to Nesvizh.

The hotel entrance was protected by two sets of heavy doors designed to keep out the winter winds that barrelled through the country when the short summer came to an end each year. On entering I walked the dark corridor to the reception where a middle-aged woman sat knitting a pair of mittens behind the counter.

'I suppose you're a Pole,' she said, handing me a form to fill in as I laid my passport on the wooden counter top, revealing the lion and unicorn of the United Kingdom's coat of arms.

'An Englishman?' She said excitedly. 'Here for work I expect?'

'No?!'

'Tourism!'

'In Hoiniki?!'

'Did you hear that Tanya?' she called out into the echoey darkness of the hotel corridor.

14

A woman wearing a bright blue sweater with the words 'love machine' emblazoned across her chest in English popped her head out of a doorway in the shadows.

'Yes I heard! English! A tourist!' she repeated.

I climbed the staircase to fumble for my room along the dimly lit corridor whilst downstairs in the reception hall I could still hear the women discussing my arrival in excited tones.

'English!'

'A tourist!'

In Soviet times there had been only a handful of towns foreigners could visit in what was then the BSSR, and Hoiniki being so close to a major nuclear plant and so far from a transiting national highway was most certainly not on that short list. And so strangers with passports of different colours were certainly an oddity in the region that was only relatively recently opened up to outsiders. Not to mention of course that the very idea that a foreigner would travel from far away to visit a provincial town in Belarus such as Hoiniki for no other reason than to take a look around was to locals somewhat incredulous, and no doubt, a little suspicious.

As the sun set over the southern corner of the country I went out in search of food, walking along Kirov Street with its boxy Soviet five storied apartment buildings and Grecian columned government offices that you see all over the fallen empire. I could have been anywhere in the former USSR, little distinguishing the town from places I had visited in Ukraine or Russia. The only uniquely Belarusian feature was the deafening provincial quietness of the place.

I pulled on door handles to government cafes that were all closed, signs informing me they would open only on Saturdays, locals no doubt not having the disposable income for such luxuries as meals outside of the home very often. The streets of the town were practically devoid of people, the exception being some elderly babushkas dressed in bright home-spun cardigans who passed time in contemplative silence on benches outside their apartment buildings. In the centre of the town I bought an ice cream from a street-vendor who had placed her mobile freezer in front of a bar where rough looking patrons sat drinking beer on a terrace locked in behind a steel cage. A police car drove slowly past, the driver watching me intently, a new face in town.

Aimlessly I continued walking the wide empty streets of Hoiniki looking for a place to eat, eventually stumbling upon the Broadway Bar which was hidden away on the second floor of a grey industrial building that overlooked a muddy car park full of rusting cars that had seemingly been abandoned. Three bored looking teenagers sat in the gloomy half-light of the bar sharing a glass of beer between them. Nobody showed any interest in the outsider that had just walked in. I ate a burger containing a type of meat my taste buds didn't recognise and then with no other entertainment options to be found I despondently headed back to my hotel along the dusty streets of Hoiniki.

By chance my walk took me past a memorial that stood overlooking a field of sunflowers on the edge of the town. A statue of a mother holding a dove in her hands behind which curved a concrete wall inscribed with the names of the villages of the region that had first been evacuated and then eventually buried in the years after the Chernobyl disaster: Radin, Borshevka, Sintsi, Lesok, Novopozhrovsk, Khvoshevka...the list curved on. Villages that had been founded half a millennium before, had weathered the storms of history only to be crushed by bulldozers and buried, taking their history and contamination to the muddy depths with them. Chernobyl was a cultural as well as human holocaust.

I continued back to my hotel but it did not take long walking the streets in the enveloping darkness before I realised I could not possibly be heading in the right direction. Instead I was somewhere on the outskirts of town having passed the last of the concrete apartment buildings and was now heading along a road lined with small wooden cottages surrounded by pretty picket fences. It was eleven at night and no cars were passing. Unsure how to find my hotel and not wanting to walk further out of town I waited on a bench outside a cottage until eventually in the distance I heard the rusty squeak of bicycle wheels. I shouted into the inky darkness at the approaching outline of a cyclist.

'A tourist?' Edvard questioned, surprised by my foreign accent as he dismounted and shook my hand. He spoke Russian with the soft pronunciation of someone born in the southern borderlands. Not as guttural as the Russian spoken in the cities, it was a southern lilt I would hear throughout my journey.

We walked back into town together, Edvard pushing his squeaking bicycle beside him. Strapped to the back-rack with an old inner tube was a small greasy sack from which drifted the smell of fresh blood.

'Meat,' he said noticing my interest.

'That's how they pay us Zone workers now. It's fortunate I'm not a vegetarian. Still, others in the town have it worse, some have not been paid anything for months. It's the 'crises' the bosses say when we ask when we'll be paid. The crises seems to be the answer to everything these days.'

Was he not afraid of the dangers of working in the exclusion zone?

'I'm alive aren't I? Anyway the radiation levels in the Zone are three times lower than here in Hoiniki,' he chuckled.

It was exactly as I had suspected.

We passed a Soviet tank perched on a plinth that commemorated a bloody local battle and then continued on past my hotel, heading instead towards the town's park. Edvard had lived in Hoiniki all of his twenty-eight years and was keen for me to see something of it before I continued my journey. After a mile we came to a stop outside a small white bricked shop that worked throughout the night. He banged on the metal door until a grilled shutter opened out of which peered the smiling plump face of a middle-aged woman.

'Let us in Valya, I have a foreigner with me. Let him see what a real provincial shop looks like.'

18

'Why is he speaking Russian if he's not one of ours?' the woman asked sceptically, unsure whether to believe him or not but nonetheless sliding the bolt back on the metal door to allow us to enter.

Belarusians always referred to each other and people from the former Soviet republics as "ours". It was a club that as an Englishman I would never be a part of no matter how many years I spent in the country, how fluent my Russian became or how many vodka bottles I polished off with the locals. When I was introduced to people in Minsk they would enquire, 'Is he one of ours?' "Oh no he's not ours, he's English," came the usual answer. And for some reason it always stung a little that I wasn't permitted entrance into the exclusive 'ours' club.

The shop was just a small square room packed on three sides with bottles of beer, vodka and chocolates with only a small corner reserved for shelves offering essential food-staples. It would be the same in every shop I visited in the country. In fact in no other country I had visited did the people have such sweet-teeth and the desire to get plastered as they did in Belarus. I always saw it as the mark of a great nation where the people had their priorities in the right order.

We left clutching a bag of plastic beer bottles and headed to the nearby town park. Edvard left his bicycle and meat-wages leaning against a tree by the entrance.

Should you not lock your bike I asked, or at least take the packet of meat. Someone could steal it. Edvard was confused by my concern.

'This isn't Moscow, things like that don't happen in Hoiniki. I never lock my door, in fact I don't even think I have a door key anymore. That's also our problem in fact, we Belarusians are a bit too obedient.'

It reminded me of the occasions I had broken minor laws in Minsk, impatiently crossing the road on a red light or drinking a bottle of beer on a tram, and the looks of disbelief on people's faces, as though they were not sure what such a rule-breaker was capable of doing next; I might take a shit on a war memorial or murder a pensioner.

An old manor house stood at one end of a gravelled walkway that skirted an abandoned factory made of rough concrete slabs which still had their rusting lifting hooks cemented into them from the time it was constructed.

'A Polish prince lived here once, he built the manor but of course that was long ago. Then the Bolsheviks came and he disappeared. Under the Soviets the manor house became a canteen for factory workers, now it's a museum.'

The Soviet government had had a habit of reducing reminders of all that happened under the old ways to something base. Churches became pig sties, palaces became worker's canteens, and the former inhabitants of both became nothing more than whispered memories as they were sent to the camps in boxcars.

We came to a newly constructed amphitheater where local musicians performed concerts in the short summer months to local families who were brave enough to withstand the attacks of mosquitoes that buzzed around constantly.

'The concerts are boring, just kids from the music school playing their instruments, but there isn't much else to do here on weekends so people come to watch. I play in a rock band but we have never been allowed to perform here despite asking the local council repeatedly. I think we are seen as too avant-garde for local tastes,' he said, barely concealing his pride at the fact he was part of a blacklisted group.

We sat on the stage of the amphitheater in the empty park under the orange glow of street lights and slowly polished off our bottles of beer.

'I used to come here regularly with my wife and daughter on weekends, we'd eat ice cream and walk around the park, there's nowhere else in town to go. But then Svetlana left me and moved to Minsk with a guy. She hasn't let me see my daughter for months so I'm taking her to court but if that fails to sort things out I don't know what I'll do...'

He trailed off lost in his memories before taking another swig of beer and snapping out of his melancholia.

'Hey, know any Russian songs?'

And so we stood on the stage as night merged slowly into morning, drinking bottles of Belarusian beer and singing the Soviet rock songs you hear in bars from the Baltic to the Sea of Okhotsk. Finally, Edvard had gotten to perform in Hoiniki's amphitheater.

As the first crack of morning light appeared over the top of the manor house where the White prince had been disappeared by the Red commissar, we walked back to the hotel, the sound of squeaking wheels and the smell of raw meat accompanying us.

'You know life really isn't bad here, you'll see the goodness of the Belarusian people on your journey,' Edvard said when we arrived back at the hotel.

'I just wish we had a bit more money in our pockets to live normal lives like you do in England. I don't think that is too much to ask for.'

With that he straightened the packet of meat, mounted and peddled off unsteadily in the direction of home. The words of Viktor Tsoi drifted into the early morning sky behind him.

FIVE

The next morning I walked to the bus station which was situated out on the edge of the town where grey concrete ended and yellow fields began. It was early but the sun was already beating down on the land making distant buildings appear to wobble in the heat-haze as I headed along the road clutching my backpack and nursing a hangover. In the station waiting room I bought a ticket at the small cashier's window from a plump babushka who had smeared purple lipstick across her mouth and teeth with the finesse of a toddler using crayons for the first time. An hour later I boarded a small yellow bus along with a handful of elderly passengers dressed in bright headscarves all heading in the direction of Loyev, a town that lay at the confluence of the Sozh and Dnieper rivers somewhere along the meandering Ukrainian border. I chose the town randomly having no definite route mapped out for my travels in the country preferring instead to see where the winds took me, boarding pretty much whichever bus was leaving next as long as it was heading roughly north.

Some distance out of Hoiniki, passing by the circular windows of the old Czechoslovakian built bus as we trundled through the flat featureless landscape of the Polesia region, there appeared small housing estates consisting solely of white bricked single-storied dwellings, planted it seemed to my eyes at least, randomly in the middle of nowhere. They looked alien in the surrounding landscape of ancient forest and bright wooden villages that had been built hundreds of years before. These were, I was told by the elderly man sitting next to me who spat sunflower seed shells into his hand throughout the journey, the estates of the internal refugees. With the villages in the far south of the country having been evacuated and buried soon after the Chernobyl disaster, the then Soviet government had hastily built these small lonely communities outside of the official exclusion-zone in which to house the new arrivals who had been evacuated away from the deadliest levels of radiation that had poisoned the lower part of the country. But despite the years that had passed, the estates with their still treeless parks and bare back gardens looked temporary, as though the residents were just passing time there until they could return to their villages. But there were no villages to return to.

The only other features on the flat monotonous landscape of rolling fields and forest that we passed through that bright morning were graveyards overflowing with welded blue-steel crosses. Perched on top of small rises in the land and more often than not sheltered by a copse of trees, they were always surrounded by a low wooden picket fence painted light blue. What I did not know then as I began my journey was that this distinctive light blue colour, the colour of the summer skies above, would accompany me everywhere throughout the countryside: churches, schools, cottage furniture, outhouses, bus stops, everything in fact would be painted this certain shade of colour that I would label Belarusian-blue, so ubiquitous was it to be throughout the hinterland. There had to be some deeper cultural significance to the omnipresent colour but I never found out what it was. Nobody I asked could ever explain it either. Perhaps I was just reading too much into it and the real reason was more prosaic; a surplus of supply at the paint factory perhaps.

Our bus continued through the featureless landscape dropping elderly passengers at remote bus stops named after the Soviet nomenclature, all the while pumping black diesel fumes into the hazy blue sky behind us, until eventually at midday we chugged into the low-slung riverside town of Loyev.

Once a part of the Polish realm before eventually being absorbed into the expanding Russian Empire with the shifting balance of powers and borders, Loyev had been destroyed by the German army on its harried retreat from Stalingrad leaving not much of the city's five-hundred year history intact. What wooden structures had survived the Fascists had been bulldozed and re-built in concrete by the Soviets in the name of progress leaving a city of low level box like grey buildings that revealed only occasional hints of Loyev's historical past.

I disembarked the bus onto the warm asphalt of the main street and entered a nearby shop which boasted an interior unchanged since Soviet times where the shelves were stocked with the same grandmotherly fashions I recognised from the bus journey, along with home furnishings such as modern sofas that cost the equivalent of at least six months pension in this the poorest region of the nation. It was hard to imagine who would be able to furnish their homes with such expensive items and yet despite the high cost of furnishings and foodstuffs there was a queue of elderly people patiently waiting for their bills to be tallied on an abacus by a young shop worker who sat inside a glass cubicle by the entrance, speedily flicking the wooden beads from one side to the other.

Afterwards I took a seat on a bench under the ubiquitous Lenin statue to eat a packet of crab sticks and watched as bare chested fisherman drifted lazily in the shallows of the river in their small rubber dinghies. Life seemed to have stood still in Loyev; no cars passed and the only noise that broke the silence of the provincial afternoon was the occasional passing rattle of a babushka's shopping cart on the cobbles. Even the nation's ever present policemen didn't bother showing their faces in Loyev in the heat of the summer's afternoon. A large perspiring drinks vendor attired in a neat blue apron stood idle waiting for passing customers but nobody appeared from the paths to buy anything. It reminded me of what the ice cream seller in Hoiniki had said when I had asked her what it was like living in a small provincial town in Belarus: 'Incredibly boring,' she had replied after a little thought.

On the banks of the river I chanced upon the recently renovated war museum but it was closed. Through the locked gates I could see a neatly polished T-34 tank which is to the

Soviets what the Spitfire is to the British, the steel symbol of defiance and victory. Instead, I headed to the town's hotel in search of a meal but its restaurant was shut too. Through the window I could see tables collecting dust in the gloom of a large dining hall.

Finding nothing else to occupy myself with and having seen all Loyev seemingly had to offer a traveller I headed back to the river bank in search of a boatman who would be willing to take me to the far bank from where I hoped to find a lift to Gomel. By the water's edge I came across a bear like man fixing a boat's motor that lay in a hundred pieces on an oily blanket. His bare back bore a magnificent tattoo of a Russian church complete with twisted Oriental spires created in the familiar blurred blue ink of the prison artist.

'A memento from Siberia,' he said, revealing a row of silver teeth that dazzled in the sunshine.

We agreed on a price of fifteen roubles and I climbed into a metal dinghy that he pushed out of the sandy shallows and into deeper water before jumping in and pulling on a thin rope that spluttered an ancient motor bolted onto the back of the boat into life. Immediately a cloud of black smoke wafted out across the surface of the grey coloured water in our wake. Soon we made it out into the middle of the fast flowing channel where river water that had flowed south from Russia splashed over the bow as the boat rose and sank in the swell, drenching us. I gripped the plank on which I was seated and leaned my bodyweight into to the bow every time the boat rose steeply over a wave, afraid that the hulking frame of the captain behind me may have capsized us. Falling into the rough waters would in most likelihood have resulted in a frantic gasping death. But the captain knew the waters well and guided us out of the rough surf and into the flat flowing channel of the far side where schools of small fish swam amongst the submerged river grasses.

Able to relax as we puttered north along the far bank towards a small wooden jetty rising from the bullrushes I mentioned the price of goods I had seen in the shop in Loyev, asking how people managed to survive in the region where there was such a large discrepancy between costs and wages.

'There is an anecdote,' he began.

'The three Slavic presidents are having a meeting and Putin says, for every hundred dollars Russians make I take twenty in tax. Poroshenko then says for every hundred dollars Ukrainians make I take seventy-five in tax. Lukashenko then says, for every hundred dollars Belarusians make I take one hundred and twenty in tax. The other two turn to him and ask how is it possible that the Belarusian people manage to pay more than they make? I have no idea, replied Lukashenko, but somehow they always find a way. Well, that's how we live in Belarus,' the boatman said, 'Somehow we always find a way.'

We pulled up on the far side of the river, the engine's propeller jarring as it hit the sandy bottom. I paid with some damp banknotes and clambered out unsteadily onto the wooden jetty before climbing up a steep grassy bank, pulling on exposed roots for support. Without a wave the boatman turned the bow back in the direction of Loyev and headed out into the fast flowing channel once again, the twisted spires on his back slowly disappearing in the frothy tops of the waves.

Alone, I joined a sandy track that headed into the darkness of the forest and followed it for a couple of hours without seeing anyone, all the while being harassed by squadrons of mosquitoes until, as the sun began to drop, I emerged into the light and passed a graveyard of Belarusian-blue crosses and then soon after, tired and with bloodied lumps up and down my legs I entered the sleepy tin-roofed hamlet of Abakumi.

SIX

I shouted a greeting over a garden fence on top of which were placed upturned cooking pots before opening the heavy wooden gate and entering the tidy cottage yard. If the sight of a stranger walking up the garden path surprised the stoutly built babushka who sat peeling potatoes over a bucket she did not show it. Introducing myself and explaining where I had come from she immediately offered me a place on her porch for the night and whilst babushka Valya headed inside to prepare tea I doused myself in the cool water from her garden well, washing the squashed mosquitoes from my body.

A middle-aged man I took to be her son was sat on his haunches tinkering with a child's bicycle in the yard. He stopped what he was doing as I washed myself and stood close, too close, staring at me mutely before the babushka came out of the house to shoo him away, tapping her temple to indicate he was mentally not quite all there.

'Don't give him money, he drinks too much as it is,' she said, 'and he'll keep pestering you for more if you do.'

With that he righted his bicycle that was far too small for him and comically cycled off towards the village as though a member of a travelling circus troupe.

I dressed and went for a walk finding a derelict building which had once served as the village club house back in Soviet times. Anything of value had been stripped from the building leaving empty rooms devoid of even window frames and floor boards. It smelt of pig shit. The Soviets had used the old pre-revolutionary manor houses as pig sheds and now their derelict Soviet buildings were used for the same purpose. The circle of history complete.

Afterwards I returned to the cottage where babushka Valya invited me into her dark kitchen to drink the tea that she had boiled on a wood fired stove decorated with pretty glazed tiles depicting simple pastoral scenes. The room in which we sat was watched over by a row of icons and dusty black and white photos that hung from nails banged crookedly into the yellowed plaster wall. A shrine to past times.

One of the photos was that of a smartly but outdated-dressed man in a wide lapelled suit holding a young child. It stood apart from the others. I asked who the people were and babushka Valya stood and removed the frame from its place on the wall before sitting and gazing at the fading picture in her lap before beginning her story.

'Sasha my son, he had opened a shop selling clothes from Poland when the system broke apart, started making money, bought a Japanese car, an apartment, and married. But It wasn't long of course before people started to visit him and demand money. That's how it was back then, he wasn't naive, he knew they would come at some point. He started paying but then that was not enough, and they demanded more, and then more. Eventually he could not afford to pay and, well....' She trailed off as though vocalising what had finally happened to her son out loud was a pain she could not bare. She dabbed her eyes with the corner of her apron.

'Thank God we don't live in those times anymore, we have Batska to thank for that,' she said, before replacing the photo to its hallowed place on the wall.

Batska which is an earthy translation of father, is the way in which almost every Belarusian refers to their president. In fact in all my time in the country it was only the official State media I heard call him by his title, everyone else just called him Batska. The reason for this folksy moniker is that despite the dodgy elections and changes to the constitution that have helped keep Lukashenko in power for so long, even his staunchest opponents would admit they have a grudging respect for the man who before becoming the president of Belarus worked on a state-farm in the provinces, in other words not a merely a man of the bureaucracy but one of the people too. Someone who understood life in the village.

Since becoming the nation's first elected president he has
dragged the country out of the dark days of Bandit Capitalism
when the cities of the newly independent Republic were
controlled by track-suited thugs with hard faces and harder
hands, and who has if nothing else turned Belarus into a well run
and orderly nation of law and order that, despite its reputation in
the West, is the envy of a lot of citizens in many of the former
Soviet Republics. Ask a taxi driver in Bishkek or Tbilisi what they
think of Belarus, and they immediately say 'Batska' and give a
thumbs up.

The reason for this lies in the fact that what the people of
these republics with their tumultuous history of revolution and
banditry seek more than anything else is civil order and stability.
That their savings will not be wiped out overnight and that the
leather jacketed thugs from the 90s will not return to the street
corners of their towns, menacing anyone weaker than
themselves. And hence, despite leaders like Putin and
Lukashenko bending constitutions to suit them, the people,
especially the older generation, feel it is a price worth paying to
have a strong man in charge who ensures that despite what goes
on behind the doors of power, things on the streets at least are
kept 'in order'.

What also plays well to large parts of the Belarusian
population is Lukashenko's refusal to bow to Western pressure
and allow non-Slavic values to penetrate the conservatively
religious country. So for example, when Lukashenko was asked
by journalists if he would allow a gay-pride parade to take place
in Minsk he replied that he would not block the idea, but on one

condition: the parade had to take place on the second of August. This caused much hilarity amongst the Belarusian people because August second is national Airborne Troops day, a day when drunken blue berets run the streets of the nation's cities and most definitely not a day for a guy to be walking up Lenin Avenue in a pink dress and a rainbow flag.

Another thing is that the Belarusian people for the most part believe that Lukashenko, despite how he goes about things, is at least sincere in his desire to improve the lives of the Belarusian people. And in that regard he has shown time and time again that he is not afraid to stand up to Russia. When asked at the time of the Ukraine crises what he would do if Putin ever tried invading Belarus, Lukashenko said that should Russian tanks ever appear on the Belarusian border he would personally go there himself and fight the Russian president to the death. And so the people of Belarus, many of whom are struggling to make ends meet in jobs that pay little or feel that they want a political re-structuring of some sort, still have a certain level of respect for Lukashenko, or as everyone calls him, Batska.

News of my arrival soon spread through the small hamlet. Neighbours came to gaze over the garden fence, discussing my presence amongst themselves as I sat on the porch reading under a dim yellow bulb that buzzed with insects, everyone wanting to see the foreigner who had appeared from the forest which was no doubt the first thing of interest to happen in the hamlet for a long time. By chance the once weekly bus service to Gomel would be leaving early the next day. And so, content that I'd be able to continue my journey quickly, as the stars appeared above the cottages and the sound of the rushing river rumbled somewhere out in the darkness, I put my book away and lay down on the old sofa on babushka Valya's porch. Her son who had returned on his little bike sat on a wooden bench in the garden watching me silently, until eventually unable to keep my eyelids open, I fell asleep under his benign gaze.

SEVEN

The crow of the village cockerels woke me as the first rays of the morning sun glimmered off of the shiny tin roofs of Abakumi. A fresh breeze swept along the muddy central avenue on which Valya's cottage stood, slamming window shutters along the street and rustling the trees that sheltered the cemetery at the far end of the road. Perched on top of a small rise in the land that afforded a view of the river below, it seemed an idyllic place to have one's bones laid to rest.

I followed a path that ran behind the back of the abandoned Soviet club house and led down to a sandy river bank where I stripped and entered the cold flowing water of the Sozh, washing the aches from a contorted night spent on the small balcony-sofa from my body. An early riser from the village stood in rubber waders blowing cigarette smoke into the morning air a hundred yards upstream, his fishing line already in the water. He nodded in my direction when he saw me and then returned to scanning the water for signs of his evening's supper.

When I returned up the path an hour later the village had stirred into life. A horse stood tethered to a garden fence post impatiently stomping its hooves, waiting to be led to the fields and the sound of well-handles and slamming outhouse doors filled the morning air. Babushka Valya came out and ushered me into the warmth of the kitchen, seating me at the table besides the simpleton who was noisily eating a bowl of porridge.

'Yura is not my son but I treat him like he is,' she said, talking about him as though he wasn't there.

'His parents abandoned him here when they moved to Russia, they didn't want the burden anymore. He's not the only one like him in the villages, they say it's because of Chernobyl but I don't know about those things. I have lived here all my life and I'm healthy. He's gentle, but he likes to drink and people take advantage of him. He has the mind of a child.'

Yura smiled inanely and slurped down another spoonful of porridge.

An hour later I waited on a wooden bench in the centre of the village for the bus that would take me north to Gomel, the nation's second largest city. Yura suddenly appeared at speed over the brow of the main street peddling frantically on his bicycle before coming to a skidding stop before me in the dried mud of the road. I presumed I'd forgotten something and he'd come to return it.

'Give me something for a drink friend...just a little money,' he said, almost pleadingly.

The sound of his voice surprised me. I had taken him for a mute having never heard him say a word to babushka Valya since I'd arrived. A large woman waiting for the bus beside me told him to clear off, raising her walking stick in his direction as a threat. No doubt long used to being shooed away by all and sundry as he begged for coins he did not protest. Instead, he smiled his simple smile and wished me a safe journey before re-mounting his bicycle and proceeding to comically ride off down a dirt track towards the swiftly flowing river.

I recognised some of the waiting pensioners from the faces that had peered over the fence the night before. They nodded in my direction smiling their wrinkled faces and continued talking among themselves until after some time a bus from the state transport company pulled up in the centre of the village and we all boarded, squeezing our bodies and bags into cramped hard seats that would offer little protection to our backsides from the bumps in the rutted roads of the region.

The driver of our bus, a dapper looking man who smoked cheap Belarusian cigarettes throughout the journey, took our money and handed out change before climbing over the gear stick into his seat and guiding us along a road that passed through small villages surrounded by forest and river, stopping only occasionally to pick up elderly passengers who stood clutching plastic buckets of fruit and vegetables by the side of the road.

On we drove through the forests and fields until coming to a stop at a barrier that blocked the road on the outskirts of an old village. Through the driver's windscreen I could see a young soldier manning the red and white pole with a machine gun strapped across his chest. A sign besides the barrier announced: 'You are leaving the restricted border zone - Be prepared to show your pass'. Seemingly I had inadvertently entered a restricted area through the back door when I'd crossed the river the previous day. It was certainly not marked on my map as being out of bounds but I doubted that anyone would accept that excuse.

The young soldier stepped onto the bus and slowly scanned our faces. Trying to avert his gaze and not stand out in any way from the other passengers I pretended I'd suddenly found something fascinating in the flat distant fields to look at, like a supermarket cashier when you enter your pin number. In the reflection of the window I saw the soldier say something to the driver I couldn't hear who simply shrugged and took another drag on his cheap cigarette impatient to continue the journey. Seemingly satisfied, the soldier stepped back off the bus and raised the barrier, allowing us to set off again towards the city.

I breathed out in relief. It wasn't that there was anything to fear, I was obviously not a spy or of much interest to the authorities but I could not be bothered spending hours explaining how I had come to enter a restricted border zone accidentally and then filling out the inevitable forms promising not to do it again.

We continued along the small back road that hugged the bank of the river Sozh before crossing a four-lane highway and following a winding road that snaked through thick pine forests that made the air outside my open window smell sweet. Set back from the road among the pines, large sanatorium complexes began appearing outside of which people milled around or were busy taking part in outdoor exercise classes, stretching their bodies to the commands of their instructors.

Sanatoriums were set up in the time of the Soviet Union to offer domestic holidays to the workers, foreign travel in those days being the reserved privilege of the nomenclature. They were usually situated in areas of beauty, on lake shores or seaside beaches, and evidently, the outskirts of cities like Gomel where they continue to entice people seeking a cheap holiday at home. Families walked along the road in colourful swimsuits carrying butterfly nets over their shoulders and rubber dinghies for the river beach under their arms in preparation for a day in the sun. Outside one sanatorium stood a small concrete statue of Lenin who stood smiling with his hands in his pockets, no doubt taking in the holiday atmosphere of the resort. I was to see Vladimir Ilyich standing on pedestals all over the country: outside universities, kindergartens, hospitals and food factories, erected as constant reminders to Soviet citizens as to who they had to thank for their daily bread.

The driver, still puffing away on his cigarettes, led us out of the sweet smelling pine forests and towards the outskirts of Gomel, passing along a wide boulevard in the shadow of huge apartment buildings that towered over small wooden cottages that had somehow managed to survive the wars and the Soviet reconstruction of the city. On both sides of the road patriotic billboards welcomed us displaying huge photos that glorified amongst other things, the beauty of the nation's countryside, the

Border Guard division and muscular Olympic heroes who grinned from up high whilst clutching golden medals.

We crossed a high bridge below which flowed the wide river Sozh where parents walked the boardwalks with their children before eventually, after passing along a street of wooden homes and buildings baring brass busts of famous Soviet citizens who had once resided in them we came to a stop on a large square outside the city's railway station.

An elderly passenger disembarked the bus laden with heavy bags full of apples which she had brought to the city to sell. I offered to help her and together we slowly walked past the fountain on Station Square, up the seemingly never ending Lenin Street with its empty cafes and book shops, and then turned down silent back roads overlooked by fine pre-revolutionary buildings before eventually, sweating in the midday heat and beginning to regret my offer of help, we arrived at an outdoor market where old women of the villages wearing bright headscarves sat at tables selling produce from plastic buckets.

The babushka nodded at a group of gypsy women loitering at the entrance to the market when I placed her heavy bags on the counter from where she would attempt to sell them to the few locals who were shopping in the heat.

'Do you have them in your country?' she asked.

'They wait for me at the end of the day and demand money. When I refuse they spit and put their curses on me. I suppose in your country they don't dare behave like that. Batska should sort them out.'

She gave me three of her apples and I left her to face the gauntlet of gypsy curses alone at the end of the day.

Instead, I headed to the city centre in search of a place to stay, eventually finding a hotel situated behind the flying-saucer shaped circus building halfway up Communism Street. Looking up at the hotel from the outside it was hard to believe the building could have been built for the purpose of welcoming guests. Built of six stories of blocky featureless design that someone had decided to encase in rough concrete the colour of shit, it was the ugliest building I had seen on my journey. However, at just $10 for a room it was cheap. The friendly receptionist who sat in a wooden cubicle surrounded by Bakelite telephones handed me a guest card whilst bored looking muscular people lazed on the lobby sofas.

'Circus performers,' she said, nodding in their direction.

'Sitting out the summer break until the season starts again.'

After exchanging my guest card for a key with the dezhurnaya in the lobby, a ridiculous remnant from Soviet days when meaningless jobs were created in order to give people something to do, I climbed the stairs, passing the children of lion tamers and knife throwers who made the carpeted landings their play areas whilst their mums kept an eye on them from large hallway sofas where they sat gossiping among themselves.

My room was exactly the same as all hotel rooms would be on my trip. Spotlessly clean and consisting of a hard single bed pushed against one wall and a desk and television set pushed against the other. In front of the windows hung transparent nylon

43

curtains that in no way stopped the sunshine from passing through them meaning that in all my hotel stays in the country I would always wake at dawn when my room would be flooded with bright summer sunlight.

I can't say I had high expectations for Gomel having heard reports from friends in Minsk who had been only too happy to leave the slow paced provincial city behind but it impressed me nonetheless.

It was an attractive and welcoming place populated by friendly locals who spent their evenings hanging out in the city's parks and strolling along the sidewalks on the banks of the Sozh, enjoying beers in the outdoor cafes that were dotted throughout the centre. Founded a thousand years before on a bluff overlooking a bend in the river, Gomel became an important trading fort from where early Slavic tribes traded pelts with the wealthy town of Kiev downriver. The fort built by those early settlers is now long gone, the city that replaced it, an eclectic mix of architectural styles. Beyond the pre-revolutionary wooden cottages and early Soviet buildings with their imposing columns in the centre of the city, the late Soviet-built parts of Gomel were a showcase of Socialist city planning. Communism street, the city's main thoroughfare, ran for miles from one end of the city to the other, boasting large hotels, department stores, cinemas, parks, theatres, sports centres and everything else a Soviet citizen could have desired. And towering above it all were long rows of apartment buildings to house them. I spent my first afternoon riding on trolleybuses that whizzed along wide thoroughfares delivering me into the outer regions of the city where a huge web of housing estates named after heroes of the Soviet Empire stood out against the ever present backdrop of the forest.

Unlike in many former Soviet republics where the old system was reviled, there had been no rush or desire to eradicate history in Belarus. I sat in a park watching pensioners play chess on Soviet Street before having a beer in a pub on a street called '40 Years Of The Belarusian Soviet Socialist Republic.' Then there were the smaller arteries of the city named after lesser known figures: Frunze, Kalinin, Okhlopkov. In fact the Soviet past was not only preserved in Belarus, it was celebrated.

Products in the city's supermarkets were sold in nostalgic mock-Soviet packaging. Ice cream wrappers were emblazoned with hammers and sickles, vodka brands were named after Gagarin and Stalin, everyday essentials were advertised as being of 'Soviet Quality'. In the evening I dined in a Soviet-kitsch restaurant where waitresses delivered plates of food dressed in the uniforms of the Komsomol and where dishes were named after leaders and events: Brezhnev's fish soup, Salad of the Twelfth Party Congress.

Television was no different. Whenever I switched on a television set in a hotel room there would be a programme set in Soviet times. It is only in the West where the Soviet Union has been completely demonised, and we therefore expect the people who lived under the system to have the same revulsion towards it that we have. To those who spent the majority of their lives under that system however, the Soviet period, or to be more precise, the post-Stalin Soviet period when the terrors ended, was one of stability and relative prosperity where work was plentiful and products were cheap. Practically every taxi driver I talk to in the former USSR reminisces about growing up in those days, of holidays spent hiking in the mountains of Central Asia or summers spent sailing along the Volga and partying in the river boat discos. Old women regularly tut at grim newspaper headlines and say 'It wasn't like that under Brezhnev'. That does not mean however that people have a desire to return to Soviet rule or a USSR 2.0, people are rightly proud of the nation's independence, it's just that what was achieved in the arts, the sciences and engineering and the simpler lives people led back then is a source of nostalgia and pride for many, especially the elderly who find the new world of dog-eat-dog difficult to come to terms with.

After some searching I found the city's Jewish cemetery. Gomel, like many towns and villages on the edge of the Russian Empire, once had a large population of Jews. Expelled from larger cities such as Moscow and Saint Petersburg hundreds of years before under the Pale of Settlement, they were forced to move to provincial towns along the distant edge where they rebuilt their lives and kept their traditions. Modern gravestones of black granite bore stern-faced etchings of the deceased contained beneath wearing their Sunday best. The more elaborate of the gravestones depicted elements of the deceased's life: a delivery truck, the factory gates, an air force jet.

Among the graves I met Larisa. An elderly woman with a bent back but full of youthful energy she sweeps the graves clean of leaves and places empty vodka bottles in the bin for the equivalent of $40 a month. It's why the country is so impeccably tidy, in fact there can be no country in the world as clean and tidy as Belarus. From the capital to the smallest provincial village, parks and roads are swept and tidied every morning by an orange vested army of elderly sweepers topping up their pensions with the broom.

'Have you visited Lesha?' she asked me, using the diminutive form of the name as though she had built a personal relationship with the deceased men and women whose graves she swept every day.

She led me to a large polished gravestone depicting a young man in the military uniform of the Soviet Army. Over his left shoulder an attack helicopter I recognised from a Rambo film fired a missile towards a barren Asian mountain.

'Killed in Afghanistan,' she said sadly, 'And over there Sasha, him too. We don't want any more war. Of course, we don't have much money here but I always tell my grandchildren that peace is the most important thing. Belarus has suffered enough already. The Fascists killed so many of us, that's why we don't want to suffer again.'

She led me by the arm to a monument that commemorated Gomel's Jews that had been executed by the Germans during the war. I studied the fading inscription which told of the night Jews were rounded up and executed soon after the invaders had arrived in the city. As I did so I heard the sound of Larisa quietly crying behind me.

47

The next day, whilst riding a bus in the suburbs of the city I met Irina Edvardovnaya. Like all Belarusians you only have to ask a polite question and they immediately pour out their life story.

'My grandfather was from Madrid and came to Russia after the Spanish Civil War. He believed in Communism, believed until the day he was shot. I grew up in Siberia but fell in love with a Belarusian man and moved here in my twenties. We had a couple of children together but my daughter is dead and my son has left for Poland.'

I told her I intended to write a book about my journey.

'Well you can write that the Government killed my daughter,' she said, her voice suddenly becoming louder with emotion which garnered looks from the other passengers.

'She was protesting in the capital and a policeman stuck his gun in her chest, right here,' she jabbed a finger just beneath her sternum.

'She collapsed and died in hospital a day later. My son didn't have faith in the government after that and claimed political asylum in Poland. He recently graduated there,' she said with a mother's pride.

'And what about you, do you have a future in Belarus?' I asked.

'No, there is nothing left for me here. I recently met a man from Syria on a dating site who lives in Prague. I hope we will marry and I can move there.'

She offered to introduce me to a friend of hers. Formerly a professor at Gomel University but now a member of the opposition, he had taken part in the protests against the government alongside her daughter. I gave her my number to pass on out of politeness but knew I would not take his call when it came.

I had spent time with opposition members at informal gatherings and rallies in Minsk but had soon learnt to avoid them where possible. Spending most of their time abroad in the European Union, I had little time for their willingness to run their country down to anybody who would listen. Instead I preferred to hear the opinions of the people who knew the country best, namely those who stayed in their homeland and struggled to find their way within it.

When later that evening I received a call from an unfamiliar number I ignored it and went for a burger in my favourite fast food joint instead.

EIGHT

One night I had a vivid dream.

I was riding one of the city's green trolleybuses. On it I saw a middle aged man wearing the same clothes I had seen being sold in the region's second-hand shops, in fact there was nothing that marked him out as being any different from the people I passed on the streets of the provinces every day. When our eyes met across the tops of the seats he stared back confrontationally, challenging me to look away. I didn't know why exactly but something told me there was a certain desperation about him. Perhaps it was the sweat running down his forehead despite it being a chilly morning in the city or perhaps it was the length of rope he clutched tightly in his hand. He disembarked at a stop that stood on the edge of the forest, somewhere deep in the suburbs of the city where concrete and nature collided abruptly and for some reason I felt compelled to follow him.

He soon left the cracked pavement and headed down a small muddy slope into the woods, following a track that meandered into the depths, away from the glances of passing pedestrians and bus passengers. I stayed a good few metres behind, always keeping his back in view, intrigued to know what he planned to do but also a little disgusted with my own excitement and voyeurism at what was about to take place. Would I try to stop him or not?

At one point he left the track and penetrated the tangled undergrowth of the woods, his neck bent backwards, his eyes no doubt scanning the trees for something suitable. I followed him into the undergrowth, snapping branches underfoot and cursing my muddied shoes and jeans as I went. It was by now obvious that I was following him, and yet he did not stop to ask me what my intentions were or tell me to fuck off. Perhaps he was glad of the unexpected company.

His movements started to become more erratic, taken more in haste as he darted this way and that across paths before plunging back into the undergrowth like an animal, searching, scanning, but there was a problem he had seemingly not considered; this forest of birch trees with their branchless trunks was no place to loop a rope.

Eventually, defeated by nature or perhaps just his own fear of the final moment when as the rope would slowly tighten and suffocate, he would thrash his body, or perhaps remembering the people he would leave behind, he gave up his search, instead taking a seat on a fallen tree trunk, still clutching his rope. Once again our eyes met but now the hard confrontational stare from the trolleybus was gone, replaced instead by one robbed of any strength and fight. I stepped forward from the trees to say something, to offer some words of comfort I had not yet formulated, but he shook his head, not wanting me to cross the muddy divide between us. Instead he stood up and walked back through the undergrowth to the path that led back to the trolleybus stop. I followed him there and watched him board the number seven, returning to whatever it was he had sought to escape.

NINE

On an overcast morning I sat on a platform bench at Gomel's central bus station surrounded by an assortment of locals all waiting to board buses heading to the villages and towns of the region. I was travelling to Rechitsa, an old trading station situated upriver on the banks of the Dnieper. An elderly man with scarred hands approached me wheeling a shopping trolley full of chunks of broken glass and mirror.

'Look at this young man,' he said, pulling out a small home-made cutting device before proceeding to slice a shard of mirror in half with the ease of a hot knife through butter.

'Only eight roubles for you, they cost thirteen in the shop.'

He looked at me, his eyes longing for me to reach into my pocket and take out some coins. He was shabbily dressed in worn-out shoes and threadbare trousers that once might have been the lower part of a decent suit that he no longer had use for. Before I could speak a babushka reading the newspaper on the bench behind me leaned over and asked him to repeat how much his implements were.

'How much! Eight roubles, that's eighty-thousand in old money! You can buy them in the shop for six. Don't buy it,' she said, turning to me and obviously indignant at his mark-up.

'Hey keep your nose out of it,' he said raising his voice and sensing the possibility of a rare sale slipping through his scarred hands.

'I'm not going to keep my nose out if you're going to cheat people,' she said whilst other waiting passengers craned their necks in our direction, eager to listen in on the developing argument taking place on the platform.

'Six roubles to you,' he whispered to me when the old woman eventually turned back to her newspaper.

I shook my head, as impressed as I was by his ingenuity I had no need of such an item.

'Five roubles then,' he finally offered in one last desperate appeal before accepting I wasn't going to reach into my pocket. Cursing under his breath at the babushka whom he no doubt blamed for his failed sales pitch he wheeled his trolley of broken glass and mirror away to perform his trick to others.

After some time the Rechitsa bus pulled into a berth beneath the platform roof from where pigeons sat shitting onto the heads and bags of the waiting travellers. The driver revved the diesel engine to announce both his arrival and his impatience to depart, sending black fumes into the crowd of queuing passengers making them cough like tuberculosis patients. Once we'd boarded and settled into our seats the driver turned and asked if everyone on board had purchased a ticket already. We all nodded and satisfied by our replies he wrestled the gear stick into first and drove out of the station.

In all my bus journeys in the country rarely was my ticket checked. I could have travelled the length and breadth of Belarus for free had I wanted to do so. It reminded me of what Edvard had told me in Hoiniki about the honesty of the Belarusian people. Often I would leave my laptop unguarded on bar room tables whilst I went to order a drink, or leave my phone on train bunks whilst using the bathroom knowing that when I returned it would still be there. I rarely locked the door to my hotel room, often leaving my wallet on the bedside table knowing the cleaning lady would be entering and never felt for a moment that something would disappear. And it never did. And the lack of crime goes beyond petty theft. Fears that we have in the West are almost completely unknown to Belarusians. Parents send their young children to school on public transport by themselves without worry and women walk alone late at night through dark housing estates knowing that they are safe. On the rare occasion that I did read about a grizzly crime in the press it was almost always committed by a Russian or an immigrant, almost never by a local.

The bus puttered along the broad avenue of Prospect Rechitsa passing the October Cinema and the city's Festival park where even at this early hour people strolled with ice creams and beakers of kvas in hand before we headed into the endless suburban maze of pre-fabricated apartment buildings where fashionable Gomolovians waited at trolleybus stops heading to the offices and factories of the city. And then all of a sudden a gape opened up in the expansive wall of concrete before us, and we slipped through it, immediately passing out of the grey to be suddenly surrounded instead by the thick green forests that enclosed the city from all sides.

We crossed the outer ring road, passing a roadside prostitute who stood alone in a lay-by waiting for early morning customers, before following a perfectly straight ribbon of black bitumen deeper and deeper into the depths of the woods. Cottages stood hidden amongst the same trees from which they were constructed long ago before eventually our bus emerged out of the shadows and into a bright flat landscape of yellow fields that gently undulated towards the horizon in all directions. The passengers on the bus dozed fitfully, occasionally being jolted awake as we hit bumps in the road on our journey through the rural landscape. After crossing the slow flowing Dnieper on a rutted concrete bridge we passed housing estates set back from the highway that were built for the displaced. Grandchildren of the evacuees played football in overgrown fields on the edge of their village and rode along dusty tracks on bicycles too large for them, before eventually on the horizon appeared the stubby industrial chimneys that stood guard over the listing suburban factories of our destination. Rechitsa.

I checked into a hotel in the centre of town and was handed a heavy key to a room which was no doubt unchanged since the day the hotel had first opened its doors decades before. Such hotels were rapidly disappearing across the former Soviet Union. Huge Intourist monoliths considered too brutal on the outside and too dated on the inside for the tastes of modern tourists and travelling businessmen were being bought up by international chains and having their dark innards ripped out to be filled instead with shiny plastic and leather in an attempt to create the illusion that you were not really deep inside the former Soviet Union at all. It was only when you looked out of your hotel room window onto a landscape of rusting garage-sheds, cracked apartment blocks and staggering drunks on the streets below that the carefully constructed illusion was broken. However, for now at least, international hotel chains have not penetrated the provinces of Belarus and so these old boxy hulks of steel and cement constructed under Brezhnev and Gorbachev, with their cracked masonry that often comes loose and thuds onto pavements and passing pedestrians below, were still clinging to life and resisting change, a metaphor for Belarus.

After a greasy dinner of potatoes 'village style' and chicken cutlets in the hotel's restaurant I walked the streets of the city aimlessly, not knowing where I was going, stumbling as I went on cracked pavements that ran unevenly between apartment buildings. Built into basements were shops that bore functional names advertising exactly what they sold: 'Shoes', 'Products', 'Flowers'.

Crossing a barren square in the shadow of a derelict office building, a woman pushing a pram containing a small sickly looking child approached me.

'I bet it's nicer where you live, look at our pavements, it's impossible to push the pram,' she said, stubbing the toe of her sandal on a raised paving stone to illustrate her point.

'How did you know I was not a local?' I asked, surprised at her intuitiveness.

I wore clothes little different from the people who passed us on the street.

'You look happy,' she replied frankly.

Katya, a tall elegant woman with features that hinted at an aristocratic bloodline, was taking her young son for his daily stroll through town past empty shops and unnoticed Lenin statues. She would be heading to a swimming pool with her son the next day and suggested I tag along if I had no other plans.

With grey skies above I continued wandering the streets until I stumbled, almost literally, upon a subterranean bar built into the bowels of a featureless government building. The bar was empty except for a gruff barman and an overly attentive waitress who hovered around my table waiting to pounce on any used napkins as soon as I placed them in the ashtray. As on the streets above, the cult of cleanliness in the country continued below ground. I tried using the bar's Wi-Fi signal but as usually happened in Belarus things were not so simple. First you had to register your number and wait for a text message with a code that you would then have to enter to get online. I couldn't be bothered and gave up which was no doubt the whole idea of the convoluted process, and instead headed back to the hotel despondently.

Two middle-aged prostitutes with hard features only slightly softened by thick make-up sat at a table in the hotel's lobby cafe. They attempted to make seductive eye contact as I waited to be served at the counter, but I wasn't that lonely yet. I headed up to my room with a couple of beers and removed the bedside phone from the hook. I'd had my sleep disturbed too many times by late night propositions in Soviet hotel rooms over the years.

On the table lay a tourist brochure printed some fifteen years ago that had been translated into English, German, and somewhat intriguingly, Dutch, the faded cover of which bore a photo of smiling women dancing in a field of wheat wearing bright national costumes. The inside was filled with random facts and statistics mostly about the region's oil industry which the editor had deemed would be of interest to the town's occasional foreign visitor. It was no wonder Belarus had an image problem abroad when even the local tourist board was so out of touch with what foreigners were interested in. I drank my beers and went to sleep.

TEN

The following morning I ate breakfast in a worker's canteen on the edge of town that was attached to a small red bricked factory. Large rusting pipes covered in torn silver insulation fabric rose from metal supports that crossed the road and snaked in and out of the building at various heights. But apart from the occasional sound of banging emanating from somewhere deep within the distant inner sanctum, the factory was silent. The stubby chimney had long stopped emitting smoke of any kind, instead a family of storks nested up there from where they perched, surveying the surrounding fields.

It was still early and the canteen wasn't yet open when I entered the heavy wooden doors, but the cook, a burly woman who told me she had worked there since being laid off from her job as a teacher, took pity on me when she realised I was from out of town, hastily setting a place at a table in the large empty hall which was overlooked by a mural of factory workers in greasy overalls. The men and women held shovels and spanners aloft with muscular arms whilst wearing purposeful expressions on their faces indicating, I suspected, that they were not merely building things, but were in fact building the future.

The cook fussed over me bringing glasses of fruit juice, fried eggs and deathly looking pink sausages.

'What are you going to eat in our town?' she asked, as though there was nowhere else to dine.

'I'm ashamed that I have nothing more to feed you with!'

I assured her I would survive, but she wasn't convinced as she watched me from behind her counter, her chins resting on her fleshy forearms, occasionally shaking her head and sighing at my presumed plight. Afterwards I thanked her and paid before passing along the dark corridors and back onto the street. A minute later I heard someone call out and turned to see her waddling out onto the canteen's steps breathing heavily from the effort before handing over a salami sandwich wrapped in kitchen film. The image that many people hold of Slavs as being an unfriendly race is completely erroneous.

few hours later I found Katya sheltering from the rain in a shop doorway with her young son near the bus station. Together we bought tickets and along with a handful of babushkas boarded and took our seats at the back of a bus that was heading to a sanatorium situated somewhere out of town in the forest. The bus departed and rode through a suburban landscape of rusting steel garages and unfinished construction projects begun in the 1980s when the government had had both the money and inclination for such things, but now after the collapse these concrete eyesores covered in protruding spikes of rusting rebar, stood uncompleted all over the country. Spiked sentinels of the past that must have pierced the soul of every pensioner who passed them, reminding them of what was, of what could have been, and what never would be again.

Eventually we joined a road that headed through a tunnel of green forest for mile after mile before eventually turning down a winding lane, passing pretty country dachas where well built middle-aged women in bathing suits and rubber boots worked on their vegetable plots. Katya wore a sleeveless denim shirt that revealed heavily bruised arms. I gazed out of the window whilst she fed her son some porridge she had prepared and imagined a story as to how she may have gotten such marks; A brutal lover called Igor who would come home from the factory at night, down a bottle of Stalin vodka and take out his frustrations at a failed life on Katya with his fists. Afterwards, filled with regret he'd rest his head on her bruised body and cry tears of regret and shame. Katya would stroke his head and whisper through bloodied lips, 'I forgive you Igor'. A sudden pot hole jerked me out of my daydream.

The sanatorium when we reached it, was located at the end of a long stony driveway covered in spongy pine needles that weaved through the woods from the brightly painted bus stop where we had been deposited. We walked the path along with the stout babushkas who carried string sacks stuffed with towels and bright swimming caps until coming to the entrance of the complex where a dwarf sized statue of Lenin painted from head to toe in silver paint stood guard. Someone had stubbed a cigarette out on the top of his bald head.

At first glance the sanatorium which was a collection of two storied red bricked buildings, looked as though it might be abandoned. Paint peeled from cracked window frames and glass panes in some of the rooms were missing. It was only the children's clothing hanging from string washing lines on upper floor balconies that indicated otherwise. Built into the brickwork along one of the walls with white tiles was the year of construction: 1964, the year Leonid Brezhnev was elected leader of the Soviet Union which had heralded the beginning of the superstate's most prosperous period when oil prices were high and the Soviet coffers were full. The sanatorium had been built and run by the town's paper factory as a place for its workers to be rewarded with cheap retreats. That was all back then however. Now in the modern post-Soviet world, the sanatorium which no doubt lacked the financial backing of the factory survived by offering cheap retreats to Belarusians from small towns who could not afford holidays on the Red Sea.

The three of us walked along the gravel paths passing well-behaved children who walked hand in hand with their grandparents. Dimitri, Katya's sullen young son, ran on ahead.

'I can't afford to buy him many things since his father left but the government pays for two swimming pool visits a month so I bring him. There is nothing else to do in the city.'

The indoor pool was housed in a large wooden building that had been constructed recently. The Belarusian government was investing heavily in sporting facilities across the country meaning even the smallest towns now possessed a sport's hall or ice rink. We may only pay you sub-Saharan Africa level wages but at least you can have a game of three-and-in I imagined the sport's minister telling the people. The three of us spent an hour swimming around in the warm waters being shouted at by the lifeguard whenever it appeared we might be enjoying ourselves a little too much before eventually retiring to an adjoining cafe for ice cream.

'Your life is like a dream to me,' Katya said after I'd told her about the travels I had undertaken the previous year.

'I'll never get the chance to see the places you talk about. Just to see Moscow or Saint Petersburg now would be something wonderful. I've not been to Minsk in five years.'

I'd been too open with my experiences. The fact was that for a thirty-something single mother living in Rechitsa, escaping the provinces was something of a pipe dream. Her future she told me, lay in finding a foreign husband on the internet, hope he would visit, fall in love and take her and Dimitri back to his country. America, Germany, Mozambique...It didn't matter where, just so long as it was away from the cramped apartment she shared with her grandmother and the boredom of life in provincial Rechitsa. Tractors and women; the country's two biggest exports.

ELEVEN

The following morning I took a stroll along the banks of the Dnieper which flowed swiftly past the northern edge of the town set against a backdrop of suburban factories and listing apartment buildings. One of the mightiest of European rivers, it was along the Dnieper that the Vikings had sailed from the north bringing with them a culture from Scandinavia that would eventually become the founding state of Russia: Kievan Rus.

I bought a plastic beaker of kvas from a seller on the river's embankment. A refreshing mildly fermented drink, kvas is sold from yellow bowsers on street corners and city parks in the hot summer months all across the country. Taking my cup of the dark liquid I joined an attractive babushka on a bench who was keeping an eye on a young blonde boy playing on a rusty swing.

Marina Nikolayevna was a retired medic who had left her southern village and moved north to Rechitsa with her young family soon after the Chernobyl disaster. She pointed to an old rusting hydrofoil that lay on its side like a beached whale on the opposite bank of the Dnieper.

'I used to ride the Rocket down to Kiev on weekends in the past. Such a beautiful city. We would walk along the Kreschatik and sit in cafes taking in the atmosphere. Kiev was a different world from the village, it was as close as we could get to feeling like we were abroad in Soviet times.'

Lesha be careful on the slide, it might have sharp edges! - she called out to her grandson who took no notice.

'I graduated from medical college, married an engineer and began working at a clinic in a small village near Gomel, that was in the Brezhnev era, such happy memories. On weekends my husband who was in the Party would commandeer a truck from the chicken factory around which the village was built, and we'd take the children to Gomel for the day. Once a journalist came and interviewed me about my work, asked me all these questions about my life as a medic in the village, journalists loved such stories back in those days, the heroic worker fulfilling their quota, serving the people. He took my photo and I thought nothing more of it but then one day my cousin phoned from the city and said "Marina have you seen the newspaper?" I went to the kiosk in the village and there on the front page of Belarus Pravda was a large photo of me. My story had been printed and suddenly I was famous!'

Lesha don't go too high on the swing, you'll fall off - she shouted out.

'Not long after that the letters started to arrive. They came from all over, men telling me how they had fallen in love with me. Letters from Minsk, Kiev, Odessa...I had so many proposals! It was the prisoners who wrote the most romantic letters of all. Of course, they did not say they were in prison but you could tell from the frank on the envelope. Well my husband didn't like all the attention I was getting, so I had to hide the letters, but they kept coming. One man wrote that his wife had died, and he was lonely and wanted to find love again. I had a colleague at the time who was looking for a man, so I gave her his address and they began to correspond. He invited her to Kiev, and she took the Rocket down the Dnieper. Well he turned out to be a crank, didn't take her to dinner but tried getting her straight back to his bedroom instead.'

Lesha put that down, it's dirty!

In the evening I waited for Katya by a bus stop called 'World Peace' opposite the war memorial. She had offered to show me around the city park and arrived half an hour late, stepping off the trolleybus wearing a short dress and high heels and saying nothing in the way of an apology. I had long ago learnt that anything less than an hour is not considered late by women in the former Soviet Union.

We headed to a well-kept park in the centre of town and walked along the paths with other young couples from the city who strolled around together talking in hushed tones. In one corner someone had set up a bouncy castle and trampoline but

71

they stood unused by the passing families. The owner sat on a broken plastic chair looking bored.

'Who has two roubles to spend on such things?' Katya said sadly.

We found a beer tent set up on a patch of brown grass near the House of Culture, its plastic roof flapped in the evening breeze indicating that a summer storm was approaching. I ordered a couple of beers, and we headed to a table in a torn corner of the humid tent.

'I grew up in a village in the south, and we were evacuated after Chernobyl,' she said, half-way through her beaker of beer. 'I suffered with my health after the disaster like most children in the village and so when I was twelve I was chosen to be part of a programme that sent children who had been affected to Italy for the summer months. I ended up living with a family in Ancona who had a son a year older than me, and we soon fell in love. I returned the following year and spent another summer with the family. Such fond memories, days by the sea, trips to the mountains, Rome, Venice... Myself and Antonio, that was his name, would spend our evenings on the roof of his house. We would look at the stars and hold hands, it was all so innocent. We talked of being together in the future, living in Italy, how he would become a successful architect and that I would become a teacher. Well of course life did not work out like that. The programme ended and I never returned to Italy again. We constantly wrote letters promising to wait for each other, I remember going downstairs in the mornings to the post box in the vestibule to see if a letter had arrived from abroad. Well eventually the letters arrived less often and then stopped arriving altogether, and I suppose I stopped writing too. I met a man after university and got married, but I never forgot Antonio. A year ago after my divorce I decided to search for him on Facebook. I knew it would hurt me to see him, his life, his achievements, but I was also curious. Maybe I still had a naive hope we would begin to correspond and fall in love again. Well he had indeed become an architect as he said he would, had married and had a child, a beautiful little girl with long dark hair and brown eyes. I didn't write to him, what would I say and would he even remember me?'

Seated at the table next to us were two middle-aged men who were silently sharing a bottle of vodka and a plate of gherkins. No doubt hearing my heavily accented Russian, and eavesdropping in on our conversation, they would occasionally turn around to look at us. I knew what was coming until eventually one of them spoke.

'Why are you hanging out with a foreigner?' he said to Katya, ignoring my presence completely.

'Come and join us instead or are you too good for Belarusian men?'

'You have a problem with that comrade?' I responded, angry at his rudeness.

He was going to say something but his drinking companion topped up his glass and said, 'Leave it Andrusha.'

The man gave Katya a look of barely concealed contempt and turned back to his vodka.

It wasn't the first time Belarusian men had made comments to a girl I'd been with, shaming them for wanting to spend time in the company of a non-native.

'I have to leave this place, what hope is there here?' Katya said despondently.

We walked along city streets in the darkness as trees swayed in the winds that were swirling through the town, making our way slowly through a dark maze of apartment building courtyards containing rusty swings and cigarette butt sandpits before eventually arriving at the five storied Kruschevka building where Katya lived crammed into two small rooms with her son and grandmother. Outside under a lamp that bathed us in fluorescent light I said goodnight. Katya put her hands on my waist and leaned in to kiss me. A silence filled the closed space between us.

'Katya listen, I have...'

'I understand,' she said testily, cutting me off before I could finish and no doubt embarrassed that she had misread the signals. I would not be her ticket out of the provinces.

'Will I see you again before you leave town?' she asked, no doubt already knowing the answer.

'Maybe,' I lied.

She turned and pressed the magnetic-key into the slot before disappearing into the darkness of the vestibule where she once collected her letters from Antonio, the clunky steel door slowly closing with a final metallic thud behind her. I turned and walked back to the hotel feeling strangely sad along the cracked pavements of Rechitsa.

TWELVE

The next morning I found myself sitting inside the city's shed-like bus station. On the wall above the ticket window was a sketch-map of the region showing the towns and villages that services ran to. I chose a name at random and headed to the waiting room that contained a contrasting mix of people: young stylish women who were returning to city universities after the holidays and the elderly people who inhabited the region's villages. There was a distinct discrepancy in the number of elderly women versus men in the country, the nation having lost a generation of men to war and Stalin and after that to the bottle. The babushkas in the waiting room wore cardigans and brightly coloured headscarves tied in knots under their whiskered chins, their stout legs pushed into rubber shoes that looked as though they could withstand any season or terrain. Shoes that defeated the Nazis. The few men in the room wore smart shiny shirts tucked into black trousers. No matter how poor a person was in the country they were always well turned out, carrying themselves with a certain threadbare dignity.

A bus heading to Minsk arrived and the young women in the waiting hall clip-clopped out in their high heels to board leaving me alone with the babushkas and dedushkas. The people of the hinterland. A man of about fifty wearing a loose bandage around his neck sat down in the vacated formica seat next to me. He pressed his finger into the bandage and plugged a hole in his throat that enabled his words to be heard. In a quiet voice accompanied by a constant wheeze of air he told me he was travelling to a provincial town to spend three months in hospital. He pointed at his bandage and raised his eyebrows as if to stay 'this fucking throat will be the death of me one day.' I could make out the contours of his bony limbs beneath his clothes. Taking pity on him I handed over a five ruble note I had loose in my pocket and told him to use it for his medicines which he had informed me were prohibitively expensive for a man surviving on an invalidity pension. He plugged his throat with his finger and wheezed a thanks. I went to use the toilet behind the bus station which was just a porcelain hole in the floor and when I returned I saw him buying bottles of beer from the station kiosk with the note I had given him. He looked sheepish when our eyes met.

Eventually the bus arrived and the man with the bandage along with the babushkas with kindly smiles hastily gathered their plastic bags and bundles and made for the door, gently elbowing each other out of the way to get a good seat on the bus. I boarded last and took my place alone at the back, spreading myself out comfortably on the row of dusty seats.

The bus left the city, passing the familiar rusting garage sheds and industrial buildings and headed north-west, towards the Berezina river in which Napoleon's Grande Armée had drowned on the retreat from Moscow.

THIRTEEN

The bus followed the road for mile after repetitive mile through the forest, occasionally overtaking overloaded logging trucks that belched black diesel fumes as they struggled to climb the gentle gradients. I lay down and nodded off into a fitful sleep only to be woken by our bus suddenly braking which threw me into the back of the seat in front. There had been an accident up ahead. After fifty metres we slowly passed two cars that had crashed head on at speed. Besides the mangled bonnets lay a large elk which had no doubt been the cause of the accident. A limp pair of feet missing a shoe stuck out from beneath a fireman's silver sheet by the side of the road. A man, bloodied and cut, crouched beside the body with a dazed look on his face and the elderly passengers on the bus simultaneously crossed themselves and muttered prayers.

I disembarked at a bus stop decorated with brightly painted Soviet cartoon characters somewhere to the south of the town of Svetlogorsk. On the opposite side of the road stood a large concrete star which marked the entrance to a collective farm.

Someone with an artistic side had carved large toadstools from tree trunks and placed them, along with a collection of garden gnomes, besides the track that led to a distant housing estate. The effect was surreal. In a shop situated at the turn-off I asked where I could find a meal in the village. A babushka queuing for bread overheard and offered to feed me in exchange for some help with her garden.

We set off along the dusty track together, passing the brightly painted toadstools and gnomes before coming to the old wooden houses of the original settlement, and then a little further on to the entrance of her estate built of identical white bricked houses. Those of the exiles. From a distance the homes had looked well-built and solid but as we entered her garden and walked up the path I could see up close the shoddy workmanship of houses built in haste. Cracks ran down an outer wall and window frames didn't fit tightly, the gaps between wood and brick having been stuffed with old newspapers to keep out the winds and snows that would soon blow across the flat landscape once again.

'Go on inside,' she said, ushering me into her home with a friendly push in the back, 'I don't want the neighbours thinking I've taken in a young lover.'

Anna Alexandrovna led me to her vegetable patch at the back of the house that was hemmed in by a listing wall that looked as though it would topple over and crush her at any moment, instructing me as to which vegetables I should pull from the dark soil and which tomato plants should be lifted and tied to the wooden frames she had constructed in her garden.

'I'm seventy-nine and have arthritis in my fingers,' she said raising a hand of swollen knuckles and bent fingers that resembled knotted rope.

It was hard to imagine how someone her age managed to keep a vegetable plot at all.

Afterwards when I had earned my keep she cooked a simple pasta meal in her bright kitchen whilst I went to the bathroom to wash the soil and berry juice from my hands. Inside there was just a cold tap above the sink. Water would have to be boiled on the stove and then poured over oneself in order to shower in the colder months. She was fortunate however. In the wooden houses of the old village we had passed there was no indoor plumbing at all meaning the elderly residents had to use wooden outhouses at the end of their gardens even in winter when temperatures would drop far below zero. It was that toughness and ability to endure the unendurable, passed down through generations that has allowed the Belarusian people to survive despite the attempts of greater forces to wipe them out.

Afterwards we sat at the kitchen table eating a meal off crockery stamped with the USSR kite mark and I asked her how she had ended up living in the exile's village.

'We were evacuated the summer after the catastrophe. My husband and I arrived on the back of a truck loaded with our furniture along with other families from our village. More than twenty big Kamaz trucks. I cried the whole way. It was hard at first, the residents of the village didn't want us here and us Belarusians are not shy to say what we think. They thought they would be contaminated by us, parents refused to send their children to the village school because they didn't want them sitting in the same classroom as evacuees. In the shop people would ask us why we didn't go elsewhere, why did we have to come to their village. And at the same time there was a lot of jealousy. Why have the evacuees been given brand-new houses with indoor bathrooms they would ask. They talked as though we were living in palaces, but does this place look like a palace to you? The government eventually had to send a face from Minsk who gave a speech explaining that there was no danger, that we were not bringing radiation to their village and eventually over time people stopped worrying about us and returned to their own struggles, and we slowly re-built our lives again, but we never forgot what we'd left behind. In some ways I think many of us felt guilty, as though we had betrayed our homes and villages by deserting them. Some people left notes addressed to their houses when they left, "don't be sad little house, we'll be back one day," some wrote, but of course none of us went back.'

After dinner, I went for a stroll around the estate. At the far end of the grassy track that served as the main road through the settlement stood a row of prefabricated cuboid homes which had been abandoned long ago, the doors and windows now boarded up with wooden planks. Three young children ran over, excited to know what the stranger was doing on their patch.

'Can you show us your phone?' the eldest of the children, a girl of about twelve immediately asked.

I handed it over and she stared at it with a sense of wonder.

'Take our photo!' her younger friend said.

The three of them lined up in front of the abandoned houses and grinned for the photo. Just then a woman stomped along the track towards us with her arms crossed angrily in front of her.

'What are you doing here?' she demanded to know.

'Just passing through and having a look around the village,' I said, surprised by her bluntness. 'Is that a problem?'

'Alright,' she said as though giving me permission to stay, but she was obviously suspicious as to why a stranger would suddenly appear in the village.

'Lena, thirty minutes and I want you home,' she said sternly to the youngest child before stomping off.

The kids invited me to play football with them on the overgrown village pitch. We headed over to the patch of grass and began kicking the ball around until after a few minutes a purple Lada raced down the grassy track before coming to a sudden halt in a dust cloud behind one of the tree log goalposts. The driver, a rough looking man in a sleeveless vest which revealed a military tattoo on his bicep shouted out the window.

'Vova, Masha, get in the car now!'

'Dad, we're playing football!' the young boy shouted back timidly.

'Vova get in the fucking car now I said.'

Vova and Masha said goodbye and with heads bowed trudged off through the long grass to their father's car.

'We are just having a game of football comrade,' I shouted over to their father, 'come and join in.'

He ignored me and instead sped off along the grassy track whilst the kids waved sadly out of the back window.

I sent Lena home and returned to the house of Anna Alexandrovna.

'I was thinking you would stay the night,' she said when I entered, 'I can prepare a place on the sofa for you. No point paying money for a hotel.'

Later in the evening we sat together on the sofa in her lounge-bedroom watching a Russian tv serial set during the war. Soviet soldiers were running at an enemy gun nest in the rubble of Berlin, being cut to ribbons heroically.

'I was in Germany too,' Anna said matter of factly over the sound of exploding grenades.

'Visiting relatives?' I replied, not realising that the events on the screen had collided with one of her memories.

'No, I was sent to the concentration camps to work during the war,' she replied, not changing her tone or taking her eyes off the screen.

'Oh...how was it there?' I replied clumsily.

My Russian, whilst having been greatly improved during my time in Minsk, still lacked the kind of subtlety or finesse needed to approach such topics with any kind of sensitivity.

'Well they didn't treat me so bad, others had it much worse. Our soldiers suffered terribly though and the Jews worst of all.'

The shrill sound of the Bakelite phone rang out from the other side of the room. Anna Alexandrovna leveraged herself off the couch to take the call, picking up the receiver with her bent fingers.

I grabbed a beer from the fridge and went out into the garden for some fresh air. The night was perfectly still, the only sound to be heard that of Anna Alexandrovna's distant voice coming from somewhere inside the living room.

The tranquillity of provincial life could be beguiling and for a brief moment I considered the possibility of starting a new life in the village. I could build a cottage, take a local wife and spend my days tending to my vegetable patch. But I had spent enough time in the wider region not to be so quickly deceived by the romanticism of the provinces. The short summer months when the land was a colourful palette of greens and yellows and butterflies fluttered through the air was merely a pleasant interlude before the snow and sleet would return turning villages into quagmires of muddy slush for months on end.

When I eventually returned to the living room Anna Alexandrovna had made a bed for me on the sofa. I lay down on the cotton sheet and fell asleep to the sound of her snoring from the other side of the room.

FOURTEEN

I spent the following days riding antiquated buses and hitchhiking through the gently undulating countryside that was bathed in a yellow light, visiting orderly towns and farming communities that merged into one in my mind's eye, little distinguishing them from one another: Mazyr, Salihorsk, Slutsk, Dovsk...all with their Soviet built hotels and thin nylon curtains, all with their well-kept parks and Lenin statues, all with their Communism and Cosmonaut streets. And all with their sad history.

It was through this region that German Army Group Centre swept after the launch of Operation Barbarossa, the invasion of the USSR, and following in their wake the feared Einsatzgruppen, rounding up and slaughtering Jews by the thousand. Children, elderly, disabled, all treated with the same cruelty. Shot, hung and burned to death. By the end of the war more than 800,000 Jews had been murdered on the territory of modern day Belarus. The non-Jewish population fared little better.

From the farming community of Glusk, another town where the Germans had ruthlessly slaughtered the Jewish population, I caught a bus to Bobruisk, arriving at the city bus station on a grey and miserable evening just as it began to rain. Kitsch plastic signs hanging from the station ceiling pointed travellers in various directions: to an empty hair salon where a bored hairdresser sat idly watching her reflection in the mirror, to a dusty bar where a friendly barmaid served warm bottles of beer and sweet pastries to village men who drank in silence. Opposite the bus station on a main road stood a large billboard showing a photo of a young child out of whose mouth came a speech bubble filled with the sad plea: 'Please come home sober tonight dad'.

Bobruisk had once been known as the Jewish capital of Belarus, Jews having emigrated to the city in large numbers from less tolerant parts of Russian Empire in the nineteenth century, finding work in the lumber business from which the city had grown wealthy. They chopped and sawed trees from the surrounding forest before shipping the planks north to the Baltic Sea ports where they were hammered and nailed into the shape of hulls for the Russian Imperial Navy. On June 28, 1941that all changed when the German Army rolled into town, and before the end of July more than four thousand of the city's Jews had been publicly shot in the main square. By the time the Soviets liberated Bobruisk three years later another thirty-thousand Jews had been murdered reducing the Jewish population of Bobruisk to practically zero.

I set off along the attractive boulevards of the city in search of a place to stay taking temporary shelter in doorways and bus stops when the rain intensified from drizzle to torrential. I had arrived in Belarus with clothes suited for a warm continental summer however this year the weather was proving to be somewhat unpredictable. On some days the thermometer had barely reached 15c. Eventually, wet and cold, I made it to the far end of Lenin Street where I found the Hotel Kujbysheva hidden behind shabby apartment buildings in a poor suburb of the city.

The receptionist sat at a desk in the lobby behind which stood shelves stocked with numerous varieties of beer and chocolate.

'We have a room but I'm not sure you'll like it, you're no doubt used to more comfortable settings. Are you sure you wouldn't prefer to stay in the centre?' she said, misjudging the level of comfort I was used to or willing to pay for.

Through a door to the left of the reception hall was the hotel's restaurant in which a band were busy tuning their instruments in preparation for the beginning of a wedding party. Immaculately made-up young women sat on the lobby sofas besides their men in their grey polyester suits. The contrast between young women and their partners in the provinces never ceased to amaze me. Men who in the West would struggle to get a date with anyone ended up marrying models in Belarus where men were a rarer commodity and thus held more power when it came to relationships.

In the hotel's vestibule, sheltering from the rain and waiting for the bride and groom to arrive stood their parents holding an ornate tray on which sat a loaf of black bread and a cup of salt, the traditional welcome in Belarus. I walked back into town in search of a meal and company, neither of which were easy to find in the torrential rainstorm that had by now flooded the town. The residents of Bobruisk had had the good sense to stay home, leaving just myself and a few sodden policemen in plastic trench coats to reluctantly walk the streets.

The restaurant I had been recommended by the hotel receptionist turned out to have closed down a couple of weeks earlier. I stopped a passerby who was running to escape the storm, but he had no idea where another restaurant was to be found in the centre of the city. Defeated I began the long walk back to the hotel, eventually becoming so soaked that there was no point in taking shelter to avoid the rain. It seemed however that my arrival at the Kujbysheva had caused something of a stir amongst the wedding guests who by now were in high spirits having had a couple hours of drinking inside of them. The groom's father approached me in the lobby asking if I was the Englishman who was staying in the hotel before ushering me into the dining hall to join the party, seating me at a table covered in half empty plates and bottles.

A man beside me asked why I was in the city and soon like a game of Chinese whispers my reply had spread along the table from intoxicated ear to ear until by the time it reached the far end my mistaken identity as a respected journalist visiting the country on an important assignment was complete. With my newfound status I was ushered from my seat and moved further along the table past empty bottles and spilled soup bowls and squeezed into a chair next to Lyudmila, a school headmistress from a nearby town who spoke impeccable English with the kind of sultry Slavic accent you only hear in spy movies. She had a hairstyle that made her look like a Belarusian Margaret Thatcher which visibly pleased her when I told her.

'An English journalist here in Bobruisk, how intriguing,' she purred through purple lips moistened by alcohol, before commandeering a bottle of Gagarin Vodka from a waiter with the confidence of someone who was used to being obeyed and proceeding to fill my glass.

'The Times?' she asked.

'Occasionally, but mostly freelance,' I lied, not wanting to ruin my reputation at the table too quickly.

An overweight man sat opposite, perspiring heavily beneath the restaurant's lights as he watched us through glassy eyes. Beside him sat a young brunette in a pink low cut dress who seemed to be doing her best to resist his pawing advances. He raised his vodka glass in a silent toast in our direction before sinking the cup of clear liquid. Lyudmila leaned close to me, the smell of alcohol left her purple lips and floated up into my nostrils.

'My husband,' she said, apparently unconcerned that he was groping the pretty brunette besides him.

'Look at the men here, not at all creative types like you,' she said, completely misjudging my talents. I liked Bobruisk, people seemed to have an inflated opinion of me.

She filled her glass with more of the Gagarin and downed it in a large gulp that revealed a mouth peppered with golden teeth.

A handful of male guests left the dining room in conspiratorial chatter before returning a few minutes later having slipped into ballet dresses in the lobby that exposed hairy legs. The band on the stage struck up a tune and the guests cheered as an impromptu rendition of Swan Lake was performed by the male ballerinas. The groom, a handsome man in his twenties wearing a military uniform, was manhandled from his chair and led into the middle of the group where he pirouetted unsteadily on the shiny parquet floor, his medals jangling on his jacket. Hotel staff poked their heads in the doorway to watch the spectacle, clapping along with the guests as the male ballerinas swirled around bumping clumsily into tables and chairs. I felt Lyudmila's claw like hand rest on my knee under the table and begin to slowly massage my thigh. She purred something in my ear that fortunately I could not make out over the loud thud of the music. I smiled at her and nodded, hoping that would be enough to stop her repeating whatever it was she had said.

At the end of the performance the band struck up a popular tune and people headed to the dance floor in pairs. A large man staggered towards our table with his shirt unbuttoned revealing chest hair as thick as the forests of the country and proceeded to lift Lyudmila out of her chair and pull her to the dance floor, manhandling her protestations with ease. I grabbed some sandwiches and took my chance to escape to my room.

Sometime later I was woken by gentle tapping on my door. At first, I thought I was dreaming, but then I recognised the sultry slurred voice on the other side.

'Arthur it's Lyudmila, open the door please... Arthur!..Arthur?!'

I pulled the blanket over my head and fell back to sleep.

FIFTEEN

The following morning I headed into town to pick up a hire car. The manager of the office had been surprised to receive my call, his usual clients being locals and the occasional émigré who was visiting relatives or searching for lost family lines. A true outsider was still a rarity in Bobruisk.

Bus travel had been frustrating. I'd speed through villages I would have liked to have stopped in and pass inviting turn-offs I wanted to explore for no better reason than to know what lay at the end of the road. With a hire car I would be the captain of my own ship.

The manager led me around the vehicle inspecting it for bumps and scratches, explaining the rules of hire which amounted to one thing.

'Drive only on main highways please,' he said, handing me the keys.

'Sure,' I lied.

I headed out of the centre of Bobruisk passing Lenin statues and war memorials before immediately getting lost in the maze of grey concrete high rises and industrial buildings on the edge of town until eventually finding my way across the Berezina river on which fisherman floated in inflatable green dinghies.

Heading south-east towards the town of Vetka, I drove on smooth roads seeing little traffic except for farm vehicles and minibuses that sped between the farming communities of the region, depositing passengers at decaying provincial bus-station buildings which had not been modernised since the fall of the Empire.

The towns and forests of the region to which I was heading were, with the exception of the official exclusion zone, the most radiated in the country. For some reason the clouds of deadly radioactive particles that had drifted north from Chernobyl on those April days had drifted over the forests of Vetka and deposited their contamination throughout the region. In fact so contaminated did this region of the country become that the few locals who remained behind referred to it simply as 'The Zone'.

A radiation map I had seen online showed the entire region sitting inside a blob of dark maroon, the colour that indicated the deadliest levels. It was a region with abnormally high rates of cancers and birth defects. Before Chernobyl the cancer rate in this eastern region of Belarus stood at 82 in every 100,000 people. After the explosion however that number had risen to 6000 in every 100,000. A devastating increase.

As I approached Vetka after a few hours of following straight roads through fenceless farmland, large radiation signs began appearing on the edges of the road. Different from the small hand painted signs I had seen further south, these indicated not only a warning but also the Caesium levels contained within the dark tangle of trees that enclosed the road, forming a tunnel of deadly greens and bronzes. More signs warned of fines for anyone foolish enough to leave the bitumen and be tempted to enter the soft bed of irradiated pine needles. And yet despite that, as I drove by, occasionally peering deeper into the woods I'd see the bright cardigans and the bent backs of mushroom pickers foraging in the deadly undergrowth.

I lunched in a small worker's canteen in Vetka, a town which in the past had had a thriving ship building industry. Steamships had been built in the riverside boat yards, shaped from timber sourced from the forest that it was now forbidden to enter. Due to the Chernobyl evacuations in which over 40,000 of the town's population were hastily relocated to safer areas of the country, the town was now nothing but a half-empty backwater town where nothing much happened, the boat yards having long since stopped producing vessels of any kind.

It felt like driving through a movie set. The buildings in the centre were in good order, but they seemed uninhabited and the streets were devoid of life or activity. A city bus passed by with no passengers on board, stopping at a bus stop where nobody waited to board. I found an empty cafe where a waitress barked at me when I ordered a coffee as though the unexpected arrival of a customer in the establishment was more than she was prepared to take and I left town soon after, crossing the river along which the steamships had once plied their trade before entering the radiated forests once again. Butterflies bounced off the car's windscreen, a hare crossed the empty road in the distance and disappeared into a thicket of wild flowers and if it were not for the radiation signs that lined the road at regular intervals, I'd have been forgiven for thinking all was well in the forests of Vetka.

The bitumen of the highway ran north for an hour through the dense woods. I drove along it until bored by the monotony of the pencil straight highway, decided to turn onto a back road that left the forest and ran through the pretty valley of the river Pokats, passing small wooden villages that lined the banks of the slow moving waterway.

In the sleepy farming village of Babichi which was just a small collection of brightly painted wooden cottages built around a war memorial, I pulled up outside the village shop in search of a cold drink. The rain and cold of previous days had now been replaced with the heat of a Central European summer pushing temperatures on the road into the mid thirties. The shop worker, an overweight woman wearing a blue apron like all shop workers in the country, peered her head over the shelves of alcohol and chocolates to see what I was searching for.

Lyudmila Borisova had worked in the government food shop since leaving school and knew every face in the surrounding villages who all made their way to her shop for supplies on pension day or whenever they'd managed to scrounge a few roubles from a neighbour. A local villager with bloodshot eyes was leaning on her counter and telling her his difficulties in finding a wife.

'What happened with that girl from Krichev you were living with last year?' she asked him.

'Dasha!? She just drank my booze whilst I broke my back in the fields.'

'You haven't done a day's work on the farm in years Vova!' a female voice shouted out from a storage room in the back.

Vova lived five miles away in a small village which had no shop meaning a long walk every time he needed to buy something. I offered him a lift home.

'Stick him in the trunk,' the female voice shouted out again from the storage room.

'See how our women are! That's why us men are so miserable in this country!'

But Vova possessed a natural level of happiness that was rare. Every miserable fact he told about life in the village with its lack of work or women was bookended by a twinkling in his eye and a laugh that revealed two rows of yellow teeth.

We had driven just a hundred metres up the main street of Babichi when Vova suddenly asked me to pull over. On the opposite side of the road two men sat on a bench outside a wooden cottage clumsily arm wrestling each other. At their feet lay an empty bottle of vodka. Vova wound the window down.

'Get in Stas, I've got a lift home.'

One of the men, a tall broad-shouldered man in sandals that revealed dirty feet stumbled over to the car unsteadily, removed his nylon cowboy hat and popped his shaved head in the open window.

'What the fuck are you doing in a car?' he asked Vova incredulously, no doubt surprised to see his friend in the unfamiliar surroundings of stitched leather and air conditioning.

We followed the twisting road out of the village avoiding a black snake that slithered unhurriedly into the undergrowth before crossing a low concrete bridge beneath which flowed the muddy Pokats. A hunchbacked old woman carrying an empty shopping bag shuffled her bent body slowly across the bridge in the direction of Babichi's village shop.

'Hey Stas have you got that five roubles?' Vova said, turning to his friend.

'I'll sort you out next week, I've got a couple days work in the cow sheds lined up.'

Vova laughed to himself, revealing his yellow teeth again. He'd no doubt heard that one before.

We dropped Stas off at his dilapidated cottage on October Street outside of which lay more empty bottles of vodka and discarded cigarette packets before driving on into the village, passing a collection of empty wooden houses.

'There used to be three hundred families in the village, now there are just seven.'

'What happened to all the people?'

'The war and then Chernobyl mostly. All the villages are dying, young people can't wait to move away. What's there to do here?'

We parked up on the grassy edge of Soviet Street that ran through the centre of the deserted village and together walked down through a glade of bright flowers being attacked constantly by insects before crossing a small wooden bridge that spanned a marshy stream of water that barely moved. In the trampled grass near a picnic table lay an assortment of empty bottles of vodka that I suspected Vova had probably had something to do with. We continued through a small copse of trees before emerging once again into the bright sunlight where a collection of wooden houses stood in varying states of collapse. Vova led me to his, the most ramshackle of them all.

'I'm practically a tramp,' he said, suddenly embarrassed, not having expected to be showing a stranger the conditions he lived in, 'but a happy one.'

He pushed open the front door and led me into a filthy rubbish strewn room that served as his living room. A discarded assortment of newspapers, empty bottles, machine parts and empty cigarette packets covered every available surface. It was a dump.

'You want tea?' he asked, searching the rubbish strewn floor of his kitchen for a kettle, but I'd become squeamish in the squalid surroundings.

Instead, I asked him to show me his garden, and relieved to get me out of his home he led me to a plot of land at the back where he levered opened the creaking door to a large wooden barn. Inside, as my eyes adjusted to the darkness, the outline of a fine horse appeared.

'Malish get out here you fucker,' Vova said, entering the barn and pulling on the chain around the horse's neck.

Malish stubbornly refused to budge until Vova whipped its rump with the loose end of the chain sending the horse charging out into the yard, knocking me out of its way and dragging a laughing Vova behind him like a manic waterskier. Once in the back garden a cloud of horse flies immediately descended onto the animal's head, smothering its eyes and mouth. Malish immediately turned and cantered back into the cool darkness of the barn despite Vova's attempts to stop him.

An elderly neighbour popped his head over the garden fence.

'Got your pension Artur?' Vova shouted out.

The neighbour nodded with a smile and Vova rubbed his hands.

'I'd invite you to spend the night in my place but you've seen what condition it's in,' he said apologetically as we walked back to the car, no doubt also reluctant to split the vodka he'd soon be drinking with his neighbour.

'250 roubles a month the local farm pays and that's for an eighteen-hour day by the time I travel to the fields and back. I'm not going to slave away for Batska or anyone else for that kind of money, and so I live like this.'

The corner of his eyes wrinkled and the familiar chuckle rose from his stomach but this time it sounded forced.

FIFTEEN (PART 2)

The road continued north through the idyllic valley, skirting the Russian border and passing through wooden villages containing more empty houses and war memorials. It was impossible not to be struck by the craftsmanship of these heroic sculptures. In remote villages of no more than a hundred houses the Soviets had commissioned works of art that could have graced large city squares. In one village I stopped to inspect a huge bronze bust depicting the faces of two army commanders killed in the region which had been sculpted by an artist of considerable talent and yet it was placed in a remote corner of the country where few people would ever see it.

At Krasnapole, a small hilly town made up of pretty turn of the century buildings and a large statue of Lenin I turned east, following little used back roads into the eastern bulge of the country that punched its way deep into Russia's western flank. The road was completely devoid of traffic that afternoon, the only vehicles I passed being a convoy of combine harvesters that were returning to the collective farm sheds after a day in the fields. A flock of storks hunted in the freshly cut fields.

Collectivisation had been an agricultural policy forced on the Belarusian people by the Soviet authorities. As the USSR was industrialised in the early days of its existence and people moved en mass from the countryside to the cities in search of work at the newly built factories, more and more grain and meat was needed to feed them. The order was sent down to confiscate the plots of land that the serfs had not long before won for themselves and to amalgamate them into huge farms that would be controlled by the State in the name of efficiency. However like many Soviet farming policies it soon ended up becoming a disaster. The farmers and land owners who refused to hand over their land and animals to the collective were liquidated or sent to the camps, and the authorities in their zealousness to acquire more and more food for the urban areas confiscated everything they could, leaving the people in the provinces to starve so the cities could eat. Hundreds of thousands of Belarusians were to starve to death in a region wide famine that killed millions across Belarus and Ukraine.

Lukashenko has kept the state's monopoly on the nation's farmland and the old system of state farms continues although the methods of collection are now not as brutal as in the past. The profits from farming that he argues would be sent to overseas bank accounts were land to be sold to foreign investors, are instead being re-distributed in the vast array of social initiatives that the government of Belarus has rolled out throughout the country. Amongst them is the guarantee of work for all

Belarusian citizens, generous maternity benefits that put other nations to shame, pensions that are in some cases paid from the age of fifty-eight and free health care and education for all. The list of benefits goes on but the nation's economy is small and hence so are the handouts.

As the sun began to set over the fields and forests on the lonely stretch of the eastern highway a monstrous steel factory appeared on the horizon belching black fumes into the azure air where it hung like an oil slick above a distant hilly town. A little while later I arrived under the black fumes in the attractive settlement of Kastyukovichi.

Driving along the narrow streets of the little town I passed young couples who pushed prams and ate ice creams in the warmth of the summer evening. A beer tent set up in a pretty park was packed with locals enjoying themselves and it seemed as pleasant a place as any to spend a Saturday night in the provinces.

A young woman out walking her dog along the tree lined central avenue pointed me in the direction of the town's hotel but when I pulled up outside I knew I would not be staying. The building had recently been renovated with plastic double-glazed windows and a neon sign that stood blinking on the roof. Outside was parked an expensive BMW with Russian plates. I had a policy in Belarus of never spending more than ten dollars a night for a hotel and so I didn't bother to stop but instead continued past the hotel on the road out of town, re-joining the deserted highway.

The road continued heading east through the flat borderlands, watched over by storks that sat perched in huge nests on top of telegraph poles. I followed the road signs which pointed me towards the last town at the end of the road: Hotimsk.

At a lonely bus stop located on the edge of the forest a lanky elderly man holding a bucket of dark coloured mushrooms flagged me down. Was he not afraid to eat food from the forest I asked as we drove past more signs alerting us to the high levels of Caesium in the woods he had just spent the day foraging in.

He spread his bony hands, 'What else am I going to eat?'

I dropped him off at a muddy track that ended at a cluster of dilapidated wooden houses on the horizon.

'I don't have anything to pay you with,' he said apologetically as he climbed out of the car, before adding as an after thought, 'unless you'd like some mushrooms?'

Eventually at sundown I passed a concrete sign that marked the entrance to the town of Hotimsk which, situated as it was in the most easterly corner of the country, felt as though it was on the edge of the known world. I drove over a bridge that spanned a grassy river bank along which teenagers sat listening to pop music in the dusk, before passing the imposing government buildings on Lenin street and eventually coming to a stop outside the town's Hotel Besid which was housed in a two-storied brick building painted with lime green stripes. It looked cheap and rundown.

'English! Are you here to meet a woman?' the middle-aged receptionist asked as she tried to decipher the Latin script in my passport.

'We have never had a foreigner stay in the hotel before, I'll have to report your arrival to the police so you may receive a visit from them,' she informed me airily, as though random police visits were just a fact of life in Hotimsk. Behind her on the cluttered reception wall among calendars and icons hung a government information poster: 'Stop Rape' it said in large unmissable letters alongside a picture of a man holding his head in his hands as though remembering some heinous drunken sex crime he'd committed in his hotel room the night before.

There was the usual endless pile of forms to fill in as always happened when I checked into hotels but the receptionist's inability to understand the Latin letters in my passport meant she was perplexed by the task.

'Is this your visa?' she asked, pointing at the photo page of my passport.

'And what does this say?' she asked with a confused look on her face whilst examining a Japanese entry stamp that she held upside down.

Leaving her to figure it out herself I headed upstairs to my room, passing more rape posters in the corridor before dumping my bag and heading out onto the streets as the sun dipped behind the corrugated roofs of the town's apartment buildings.

In a small park in the centre of Hotimsk over which towered a large Ferris wheel that no longer turned I asked a couple of teenagers if there was a decent place to eat in town.

Liza and Olya were on their usual evening walk around town which they took every night of the week, every day of the year.

'There's literally nothing else to do here except walk the streets,' Liza said, laughing at the absurd monotony of provincial life.

The place they took me to turned out to be nothing more than a small metal kiosk with a steel-grilled window through which a woman served microwaved pancakes filled with cheese and mushrooms.

'They're delicious don't worry,' Olya assured me, sensing my disappointment at another evening without a decent meal inside me.

After weeks of surviving mostly on cheap packets of dried noodles that kindly receptionists had prepared for me I was desperate for something more substantial.

'The woman working behind the window is our physics teacher, but she runs this place on the weekends.'

We waited in line with a handful of young locals who occasionally looked around to study me more closely, not quite sure what to make of the sudden appearance of a stranger in their town, whilst the girls bombarded me with the questions I'd answered a hundred times in the country: Why was I here and not somewhere else? Did I like Belarusian girls? Was I not afraid of travelling alone?

Eventually our turn came and the physics teacher handed me a steaming pancake through the grill. They were right, it was delicious.

The girls invited me to join them on their usual evening walk around Hotimsk to show me the few sights the town possessed, and with nothing else to do I accepted.

We headed off, walking back along Komsomol Street, past the Soviet Ferris wheel that didn't turn and then left the centre of the town along dark streets before heading onto 50 Years Of The USSR Street, the three of us squeezed onto the narrow pavement.

'Don't walk on the road, you'll get a fine by the police,' one of the girls said in the darkness as I stepped onto the bitumen.

As we walked they continued to ask me questions about my trip, intrigued to know what I thought of Belarusians. I told them that I found Belarusians overly wary of me in the beginning but seemed to relax once they realised I spoke Russian.

'Yes we can't imagine why a foreigner would come to Belarus so if we see one I suppose we would automatically think uh oh what's he up to? However, you're not the first foreigner to visit our town. Two years ago we had a man here from China who married a local girl. She met him on the internet and now they live in his country.'

No matter where you go in the world there's always some dude who has been there before you. And shagged a local.

We carried on over a bridge before turning right along the riverbank with its war memorial shaded by willow trees, before passing the town's imposing government hospital which seemed absurdly large for such a small provincial town.

'There must be a lot of ill people in Hotimsk,' I said.

'Yes, many,' Liza replied flatly, obviously not catching the irony in my statement.

We hurriedly passed the town's police station where a couple of officers stood smoking on the porch and then crossed another bridge back over the river before eventually arriving back in the centre of town where we had begun our walk just twenty minutes earlier. And that ladies and gentlemen was Hotimsk.

The three of us sat on Lenin's plinth in the darkness of the town's central square.

'Can you say something in English for us, we have never heard a native speak it,' one of the girls said.

I introduced myself, and they both burst into fits of laughter. They had not understood anything I had said.

'You don't even understand the word hello?' I asked surprised. 'What English words do you know?'

They contemplated the question for a few seconds before Olya replied, 'Motherfucker,' and they burst into laughter again.

'How do you cope with the boredom here?' I asked. Liza, the more thoughtful of the two answered.

'We walk around town and take photos of each other for our social media pages, hang out with friends. What else can we do? What we really want is a social club of some sort, ours closed down years ago. If there was a club here I might never leave. I love my town despite the boredom, and I don't believe we should feel ashamed that we live in a place with no McDonalds or shopping centres. We only have 7000 people here so of course there is not much to do, but we keep up with Moscow fashions and slang through television and internet. At least our town is safe, not like the towns over the border. Anyway I will go to Gomel after the summer to study, it will be more interesting there. I'll tell you something about Belarusian people though, we are very patriotic and feel very connected to the places where we grew up. I can't imagine leaving my country like the girl who married the Chinaman did. Despite the problems, I want to stay.'

Alarms went off simultaneously on their phones, their screens suddenly illuminating us in the darkness of the park. It was exactly a quarter to eleven, meaning they had to go home.

'If we are out on the streets after eleven our parents will get fined by the police since we are under eighteen. It makes no sense of course since we are only going to go home and sit on the internet for hours. It would be better to be out here with friends.'

We walked back along Cosmonaut Street caught in a stream of teenagers all rushing home before the curfew and fines, before eventually arriving at the green striped Hotel Besid. Low-wattage light bulbs lit rooms on lower floors whilst on the upper floor a broken window slammed in the wind that indicated another storm was going to blow through the region. The girls offered to show me the local history museum and the town's church the following day if I stayed on in the town but I couldn't take another day in Hotimsk.

On entering the lobby the receptionist handed me my passport.

'The police called, said you should go report to the station at 9am. You're not in trouble don't worry.'

I went up to my room and climbed under the coarse blankets of my bed, hoping I'd not become another rape statistic of the Hotel Besid.

SIXTEEN

The grey half-light of a provincial dawn filtered through the nylon curtains waking me early from a night of strange dreams. Outside the window rain fell in vicious droplets the size of kopeks onto Lenin Street from dark clouds that blanketed the eastern sky. In a bathroom of cracked tiles I showered and then left the hotel, passing the sleeping receptionist in the office.

Not having any desire to waste time at the police station I exited the town, instead joining a road heading north-west and passing through farming communities and villages seemingly as old as the land itself.

Rainwater streamed off apartment building roofs, gushing from overflowing drainpipes in mini tsunamis that turned village roads to muddy streams of gravel and debris. Early-risers walked to village shops housed in buildings encased in yellow bathroom tiling with heads bowed against the rains that pounded them from angry skies above.

I stopped to buy food at a petrol station situated somewhere on the gloomy outskirts of Klimovichi where a pretty young cashier lay sleeping on a camp bed behind the counter. I quietly placed the coins for some chocolate bars beside the till and left without waking her, driving on for hours ensconced in the warmth of the car whilst outside in the morning twilight a bleak landscape of sleepy grey towns and sodden villages passed by the windscreen like a sepia movie reel. It was hard to imagine someone spending a lifetime in such places, surrounded as they were by nothing but fields and forest.

Slowly however as morning came the towns began to stir into life. In this, the most Sovietized region of the country, buildings had slogans built into their brickwork: Glory to the Worker's Party, Celebrating 40 years of the Belarusian Soviet Republic, World Peace! The entrances to villages and collective farms were often marked by hammers and sickles built of concrete and steel. Sometimes they had been hidden behind plywood boards on which now were printed advertisements for farm products, but they were still there, hidden beacons of the past. Outside some of the larger towns stood the elevated remains of the towers from where once upon a time officers of the USSR's traffic police had kept a vigilant eye on people across the empire. Cars bearing distant number plates entering a town would have been stopped, papers checked and questions asked: Where were you going? Who were you meeting? But now they stood empty, the window panes long broken, people no longer needing to explain their movements, unless you happened to be a tourist in Hotimsk.

I had the road to myself that Sunday morning, awake but at the same time feeling as though I was in a dream, as though what passed by the window, the ancient wooden villages, the provincial people in their old-fashioned clothing and rubber boots, the brooding landscapes, were not quite real, and that if I opened the window and let the fresh morning air hit my face I would somehow snap out of it and the mirage I was witnessing would melt from view. But I did not want it to, instead I wanted it all to continue for as long as possible, to drink it all in, notice every detail, the sounds and smells, knowing that I was unlikely to ever return and see it again.

On and on I drove for hours, intoxicated by the beauty of the land, ignoring the instructions of the car hire manager, avoiding main roads as much as possible and instead taking rough turn-offs that headed through dark forests and yellow farmland, following gravelled tracks through small villages composed of nothing but clusters of dimly lit houses surrounded by picket fences that looked forlorn beneath the grey skies. Old village club houses built in the decades that bookended the war stood derelict. Sometimes I would leave the car and explore them, forging a path through the wet grass and stinging nettles that had formed a barrier around the disused buildings, guarding them from all but the most inquisitive. Pinned to the walls inside some were the peeling remains of lists of upcoming social events from decades past, debates, political speeches and movie nights. I'd try to imagine the weekend get-togethers that were held there when villagers would gather from the surrounding farming communities to dance, fight and flirt, all the while taking part in a huge social experiment behind closed doors, away from the prying eyes of the West.

I criss-crossed small rivers on rarely used bridges that creaked under the unexpected weight of something heavier than a horse and cart, following roads through gentle rolling hills just a mile from the Russian border that loomed out there beyond the horizon, visible momentarily between smeared swipes of the windscreen wiper. Often a road came to a dead end where once a village had stood but where now there was nothing, the only clue to lives having been lived being a lonely graveyard containing rows of Belarusian-blue steel crosses. I passed through towns built before continents were discovered: Slavgorod, Cherikov, Krichev, towns that Vikings founded, Mongols sacked, Poles conquered and Russia consumed, situated on bluffs that overlooked meandering rivers bearing Sumerian and Scythian names untaught in western classrooms. Families travelled to Sunday markets by horse and cart, sheltered from the incessant rains under plastic sheets or squeezed together into the dry cabins of their tractor, blocking the driver's view of the road. Occasionally I passed destroyed churches which had been smashed by the Party in an attempt to crush the old ways, the broken bell towers now inhabited by storks which returned in pairs from southern Africa every year to raise their young before departing again as the cold winds returned. In one village situated in a remote river valley stood a red bricked psychiatric hospital outside of which patients in striped hospital pyjamas wandered along the empty village road watched over by orderlies who called them back when they stumbled too far from the hospital gates.

On I went, deliberately losing myself, heading further and further off the map and penetrating the dark woods, only stopping occasionally to enter small wooden shops in remote settlements. I would ask shopkeepers which village I was in, and they would stare back at me as though I was from another world. I was.

I had bought a road atlas in Bobruisk but it was of little use. Belarusian cartographers had a habit of marking things in the wrong place, deliberately or through incompetency I could not tell. Roads that were supposed to lead in one direction instead headed in a completely different one, rivers I expected to cross seemed to not exist at all. But on I went, occasionally stopping to strike up a conversation with a villager who would invite me into his wooden home to share a bottle. It would be easy for outsiders to judge Belarusian men for their drinking, but living here in the bleak landscape of decaying villages and with futures that consisted of nothing more than a hard life working on the farm, every man had a right to seek his own solace wherever he chose. I would have made the same choice.

And then at midday the town of Gorky appeared on the horizon. A pretty conurbation of winding streets along which people walked wearing clothes adorned in the colours of the national flag which was popular attire throughout the country. In a cafe I struck up a conversation with a young guy who told me he was waiting for summer to end so the female students would return to the town, and he'd at last have something to do in the evenings. And there, finally satisfied that I had seen something of the provinces and had witnessed, however briefly, a part of Europe rarely seen by outsiders, I turned the car south, leaving the town on country roads that led back towards the irradiated forests of Vetka.

SEVENTEEN

N ear the town of Slavgorod, which stood on a green bluff overlooking the forested banks of the Sozh, the grey clouds finally parted, revealing the sun and bathing the land in bright golden light which began drying out the villages and towns of the region. A huge wind turbine visible from miles around appeared on the hilly horizon, towering over the valley, the modernity of its sleek steel design jarring to the eye in the landscape of wooden houses built centuries ago. An old woman sweeping a war memorial in a village stopped and stared as I passed by.

The cult of the war was still as strong as ever. People placed bumper stickers on their cars with the slogan 'Thanks Grandad for our freedom,' and every time I switched on the television half the channels were showing war films or serials set in the time of the German occupation. In every town two things took centre stage, Lenin and the war memorial, and it is easy to understand why. Whilst Britain lost less than one percent of its population to the war, in Belarus a quarter of its people perished, the highest percentage of any country, leaving no family untouched by tragedy. In one small border village I stopped to read the inscription on a memorial which read: 'From this village 379 people left for the front. 349 did not return.' It was the same in every settlement I passed through. Used as slave workers or simply murdered, the Belarusian population suffered so much under the occupation that when the war ended the small Soviet republic was given its own seat in the United Nations. An acknowledgement for its disproportionate suffering.

After eight hours at the wheel I joined national Highway 38 that once again took me south along the fenceless Russian border. Along a lonely stretch of the road and far from any town or village, I passed a turning that led off from the deserted highway before quickly disappearing into the wild undergrowth that had enveloped the road. Intrigued, I ignored a radiation sign that forbade entry and followed the stretch of cracked asphalt passing through the tangle of bushes that grew across the entrance, driving over weeds and saplings that made a whipping sound against the windscreen as I drove through them.

After a few hundred metres, rising out of the grasses at the side of the road appeared a concrete war memorial, its faded red and white hammer and sickle standing out against the green landscape in which it stood. I pulled up and left the car, walking through the deadly vegetation of wild flowers to read the names inscribed upon it. Over one hundred victims remembered but one family name written over and over: Gromyko.

I returned to the car and continued on along the cracked road for a couple of miles through a wild landscape dotted with abandoned farm buildings, determined to stop only when I doubted the car's ability to return to the safety of the highway. Suddenly out of the long grasses appeared two half starved dogs excitedly wagging their tails and bounding alongside the car as I continued slowly forging a path through the nettles and prickly plants to whatever it was the road had once led to. On I drove beside my two companions until suddenly the torn concrete beneath the wheels abruptly ended and I drove into a grassy square in the far corner of which, on the edge of the forest, stood a solitary wooden cottage.

The emaciated dogs jumped up at me licking my hands as I left the car and entered the garden of the cottage, peering through a back window to see if someone was home. Despite the squalor inside it seemed someone was indeed still living there, empty milk bottles and dirty crockery lay on a kitchen table. I tapped on the glass and shouted out a greeting that pierced the silence of the deserted land but no answer came back and having nothing with which to feed the dogs I returned to the car and drove back towards the highway watching the dogs disappear back into the tall grasses in my wake.

As night fell I reached the sleepy town of Chechersk that lay at the end of the highway. A policeman pointed me to the town's hotel, an ugly Soviet construction situated on the corner of Gagarin street.

'Check out the October bar,' he said when I asked him where people went on Sunday evenings in the town, 'but be careful, people like to drink here.'

EIGHTEEN

My hotel room contained three single beds and a fridge that buzzed like a swarm of bees. To escape the noise I headed out in search of the October Bar, a distant thud of music leading me there without the need to ask directions. As I entered through the glass doors and crossed the empty dance floor, illuminated by a colourful spectrum of disco lights, the patrons in the bar stopped their conversations and turned to stare in unison at the strange apparition of a foreigner in their club, nudging each other to make sure their friends got a good look and confirm that they were not imagining it. I found an empty table in the corner.

A heavy hand soon tapped me on my shoulder.

'Where are you from friend?'

I turned to see a powerfully built man sitting with his arm around a pretty blonde woman.

'London,' I lied. I'd given up on explaining to people where my provincial home town was.

The man motioned for me to join him and the girl at their table. He was already well on the way to being drunk and the girl looked annoyed by the fact that my presence would extend the Sunday night drinking session even longer. We ordered a carafe of vodka and the blonde rolled her eyes.

Sasha worked in a factory by day and trained at the local powerlifting club by night. We could go there and see it now he offered but I wasn't sure if he meant the factory or the weights room and neither option sounded appealing at ten at night. Instead, he suggested taking me to the city's war memorial which sounded only mildly more interesting. The three of us left the October Bar, stopping to buy beers at my hotel's reception along the way despite his blonde companion asking him not to.

'It's brewed in the region,' Sasha said, ignoring her and passing me a bottle.

'What do you think of it?' He asked.

I took a swig.

'It's shit,' I replied honestly.

'Yes,' he agreed, 'nobody here drinks it.'

The war memorial was located in a small park in the centre of the town. In the dark as mosquitoes attacked us, we stood and toasted fallen soldiers with the local beer. Sasha was beginning to slur his words and the pretty blonde kept nagging him to stop drinking and take her home until eventually he had had enough.

'Shut your mouth or go home, I'll drink as much as I want,' he said firmly, giving her a look that said 'don't embarrass me in front of someone who isn't ours.'

She crossed her arms and sighed loudly to show her annoyance but didn't reply. Sasha then began a monologue about the war and I zoned out.

I had been mentally working on a movie script during my trip to pass time on monotonous bus journeys. It was a spy thriller set somewhere deep in Belarus and was almost complete but the part I was struggling with was where to set the final climactic sex scene between the two main protagonists, an American professor who was on the run from the KGB for uncovering a dark national secret and a local raven haired beauty who was risking her freedom to help him escape. And as the pretty blonde rolled her eyes and dramatically sighed each time another bottle of beer was opened and Sasha rambled on and on about the war to no-one in particular, I realised that the eternal flame of a war memorial would in fact be the obvious choice. Naked intertwined bodies writhing in the throes of passion, illuminated in the dark by the flickering of the flame, and all taking place beneath the defiant gaze of a bronzed muscular soldier charging to a certain and heroic death. Maybe a light snow falling for that final atmospheric touch. Coming soon to cinemas near you.

'Can you explain something to me,' Sasha said, the sudden lucidity of his voice bringing me back.

'Why do you guys in the West hate us so much? What did Russia ever do to America or Britain? All we ever did was die in

Europe's wars and yet now we are treated worse than Arabs who you let into your countries without even having passports. I tried getting a visa to visit my sister in Germany last year and was refused but an Afghan gets given a free apartment in Munich. Why is it like that?'

I had no answer.

NINETEEN

It was dawn when I was woken by bright sunlight flooding into the room and the sound of a tractor engine revving in the yard behind the hotel. Sasha's girlfriend had eventually given up on persuading him to go home with her and with one final dramatic sigh and roll of her eyes as another beer bottle was opened had walked off into the darkness of the night leaving us both at the memorial to continue drinking.

We had returned to the October bar where we found some friends of his from the powerlifting club who were entertaining a table of girls from a local college. After that my memories of the night faded, appearing again only fleetingly as hazy snapshots through the fog of a hangover. I remembered being on the dance floor with a tall red-headed student, and then vaguely of being in a basement gym surrounded by barbells before finally, in the early hours of morning, I had somehow ended up next to the war memorial again but this time with the red-headed student from the October bar. I washed my face in the cold water of the bathroom and hoped that the final inevitable memory of the night would not return.

Wanting to escape the incessant sound of the tractor engine I checked out of the hotel and headed to the town's supermarket joining a queue of early morning customers queueing for groceries where I bought two large packets of sausage meat and a bottle of vodka before heading north out of town, re-tracing my route along the road I'd driven the day before, passing half derelict towns that in the darkness of the previous evening I had not fully taken in except in dark silhouette but which now stood out depressingly clear in the bright sunshine of the summer's morning.

The wooden houses of the semi-inhabited villages I passed by were well cared for, their timbers painted Belarusian-blue and gardens well tended, but the brick-built government buildings were long closed and boarded up, seemingly never to be put to any kind of use again. Subsidies that the Soviet government had once upon a time provided in the provinces had long since disappeared with the new harsh economic realities of post-independence Belarus. Kindergartens, medical clinics, cinemas and village club houses, were all long closed and derelict, left standing in a sea of weeds and nettles in villages and towns that straddled the southern end of the highway. People now had to travel to larger towns for such necessities. 'For rent' signs were painted onto industrial buildings as I had seen in every town throughout the region but there would be no takers despite the fact that there was an educated and hardworking populace waiting to do something constructive, sick of working on the state farms for subsistence level wages.

After thirty miles I came to the turn off I recognised from the day before and once again ignored the no entry sign and passed the war memorial with its list of names before driving for a couple of miles through the young saplings and foxgloves until once again reaching the lonely cottage in the clearing where I whistled and waited, but this time the dogs did not appear. I took the sausage meat from the car and walked across the empty glade putting my head to the dirty glass of the kitchen window of the house, cupping my eyes and peering into the ramshackle room. Suddenly from the shadows of the room appeared half a face and I jumped back in surprise.

I waited on a garden bench until after some time an emaciated old man appeared in the doorway of the cottage dressed in a check shirt that was frayed to the point of falling apart revealing protruding ribs beneath. When he stepped out into the light I could see that half his face had been eaten away by some disease, his right eyeball and a large part of his nose were missing, rough scars from the surgeon's knife having replaced them.

'I've brought your dogs meat,' I said, embarrassed to say such a thing to a man as malnourished as he was.

'They're out in the fields,' he told me, leading me to the front of the cottage and clapping his bony hands to alert them. The noise of bone hitting bone travelled a few yards and dissipated into the silence of the Zone. We sat on a bench under an old oak tree, its exposed roots disappearing under his house. I took out the vodka bottle and poured a generous measure of the clear liquid into a glass that the old man had fetched from the tall grass behind a fence post.

'A stranger out here is a rare thing so let's drink to our meeting,' he said knocking back the drink in a large gulp and motioning for me to fill the glass again.

'Were there houses here before?'

'You're in the middle of the village, all around here were houses, some were two stories tall and built of concrete. Over there was the shop, and there was the club house,' he said, pointing to a void on the edge of the grassy square.

'It all got knocked down and buried after Chernobyl.'

'Why did he not leave along with the others?'

'They asked me to, offered me an apartment in town, but I was born here and didn't want to leave. I remember the day the Fascists appeared from the forest over there.'

He jutted his chin at a dark line of trees on the horizon.

'I was seven years old. The memorial you passed has the names of over fifty members of my family written on it.'

'You're a Gromyko,' I said, remembering the name.

'The last one.'

He had not always lived alone. He told me of a wife and married life in the village in Soviet times when there was plenty of work and on weekends people would gather in the club house to watch the latest Soviet comedies on the projector screen. But that was another life altogether, before the evacuations began and the farm was closed after which just four families had stayed on along with an abandoned assortment of cats and dogs. His wife was eventually diagnosed with cancer in her spine and became paralysed over time. He nursed her for years in their wooden cottage until the end came, and then the other neighbours passed on and now it was just him and his dogs left. The last survivors of the village, all living on a basic rural-pension of less than $100. Once a month he would walk through the forest to the highway where a government shop-truck would stop and sell him the few essentials he could afford.

'Every year Batska says to the people "look I'm giving you five roubles more on your pension," but then the prices in the shops just go up immediately.'

One of his dogs appeared, bounding out of the woods and running up to us wagging its tail excitedly, smelling the packets of sausage meat on the bench beside me. I opened a kilogram slab of the grey coloured meat and the dog snatched it from my hand before I could place it on the ground, devouring it in three huge choking gulps. The old man sat silently watching the dog greedily fill its belly. I handed him the remaining pack of meat.

I took out my phone to photograph his house, and he immediately turned his face away from me, ashamed perhaps by its grotesqueness. Maybe that was another reason why he continued to live alone at the end of the road with nothing but his starving dogs for company, far from the eyes of others.

As I prepared to leave he told me of a nearby church that had been built centuries ago, explaining how to find the track that led to it from the highway. It was Sunday and the few remaining residents from the surrounding villages and hamlets would be attending the service. We made a final toast to our unlikely meeting, knocked back another large shot of vodka and bit into a tomato he had grown in the same soil that contained so much of his family's blood.

TWENTY

The road twisted north under an azure sky. I drove through pasturelands and forests for mile after unchanging mile until finding the stony turn-off that led towards the church which was situated a stone's throw from the Russian border. Villagers riding on horse and carts and old-fashioned motorcycle sidecar combinations headed along the track in their Sunday best lost in clouds of road dust. After a mile a magnificent church announced itself on the horizon, its planked steeple towering over the flat eastern borderlands of the Zone. Built of wood and painted bright blue it dazzled brilliantly in the sunshine. I parked and joined the babushkas in their bright headscarves who stood outside the entrance of the building crossing themselves in the Orthodox fashion whilst their husbands removed their farm caps and bowed their heads before entering the church through the large wooden doors. I followed.

The service had already begun and people stood murmuring prayers whilst crossing themselves repeatedly below the smoke stained icons that covered every inch of the walls. I took a seat on a bench at the back alongside some elderly babushkas to watch a spectacle that was no doubt little changed since the religion was brought to the region.

The congregation was mostly made up of people with the strong weathered faces of the farm, thick hands and stout arms used to manual labour. They stood in the nave under oil paintings depicting scenes from the Bible whilst in the transept stood a golden altar and beyond that the chancel from where behind the thick wooden doors deep male voices could be heard chanting. People waited patiently for the priest to emerge whilst up above the congregation on a wooden parapet accessible only by a steep wooden ladder, stood six babushkas in headscarves singing Slavonic hymns in their soft Belarusian accents.

Eventually two elderly men, bearded and wearing dirty golden robes, appeared from the chancel looking as though they had stepped out of one of the oil paintings that surrounded us. The babushkas up high in the parapet sang louder, their shrill voices filling the space above them, drifting up high to the eaves which were decorated with paintings of the apostles shrouded in the light of golden halos. Then as the suspense built, the priest solemnly appeared in the doorway wearing a fine tunic weaved with golden threads. The congregation bowed and crossed themselves and muttered prayers in quiet whispers as he stepped forward and began reading the liturgy before they shuffled towards him to taste the holy water which he poured into their mouths from a golden spoon. A young mother held a child in her arms whose body was the size of a toddler but who possessed a head no bigger than a newborn. Its tongue lolled uncontrollably out of its mouth upon which, when brought before the priest, he solemnly poured water from the golden spoon. Looking around to study the people waiting for the blessing more closely, I noticed that many were afflicted in some way: stumps, limps, a dwarf. The Church and God no doubt where they placed their hope, hope that the afterlife would not be so cruel as the present.

When the last of the congregation had drunk from the golden spoon, the priest and his bearded escorts slow-walked back to the sanctum of the chancel, closing the doors behind them with a dramatic final thud. The babushkas in the parapet lowered their voices and murmured prayers, and feeling like an intruder I slipped away through the creaking doors of the church and drove back through the irradiated forest towards Bobruisk.

TWENTY-ONE

A couple of days later I boarded the early morning Minsk-Kherson Express from Bobruisk. Outside the compartment window the world disappeared into the mists that floated through the woods and grassy clefts in the pastural land. The dimly lit dormitory wagon was full with families heading to resort towns along Ukraine's Black Sea coast, an eighteen-hour journey to the south. Children used the bunk beds as climbing frames and chased new-found carriage companions up and down the corridors in excited games of tag.

A young married couple sat on the opposite bunk holding hands tightly. Vladimir, a pale skinned young man, had just been reunited with his wife after serving a three-month sentence for taking part in an anti-government protest. They were heading to Kiev from where they planned to apply for visas at the American embassy and begin a new life in Seattle where Vladimir had distant relatives. He poured some juice into a plastic cup and handed it to me.

'I hope we can return one day, I don't want to leave my country but with Batska in charge there's no future for us here. Just look how beautiful Belarus is,' he said, turning to the misty world that raced by outside the carriage window.

His young wife began to cry quietly.

'There, there my little rabbit, don't cry,' he said to her tenderly, 'It won't be so bad, we'll soon be swimming in the Pacific Ocean.'

With that she let out a sob that forced a large snot bubble out of one of her nostrils.

'I worked in a government office,' he said, handing his wife a tissue, 'and when election time came our boss gave a speech telling us all who we had to vote for. I made my thoughts known, perhaps a little too strongly, and it caused something of a scandal. Not long after I lost my job. With nothing to lose I joined the protests where I was arrested. Well you can see why I don't see a future here.'

The gentle swaying of the carriages rocked me off to sleep until I was shaken awake by the matronly carriage attendant a couple of hours later as the train emerged from the mists and passed over a wide river that flowed silken and swift beneath us. The train rattled its way through the rusting industrial outskirts of the city until coming to a stop in front of Gomel's palatial railway station with its chandeliers and Lenin statue. I stepped onto the platform, fighting my way past families in beach wear eager to board and begin their holidays, and headed back along

Lenin Street to the familiar shit coloured concrete of the Hotel Circus.

With my visa soon coming to an end I had time to make one final journey in the region. I spread my map out on the ketchup covered table in Mega Burger, a local fast food chain which had become my second home in the city. However despite my repeated visits and often being the only person spending money in the place, not once did the girls serving behind the counter acknowledge me in any way or offer a smile. It was something I had noticed throughout the wider region, the more you frequented a place the more the staff resented your presence. In fact if you frequented an establishment too often the staff would become openly hostile towards you.

If the map could be trusted then the town of Korma was situated somewhere upstream on the banks of the Sozh, standing on the western edge of the irradiated Vetka forests. From there, heading east out of the town, the map showed a small road that crossed the river and penetrating deep into the woods before ending abruptly at a small cluster of villages far from anywhere. Beyond that the map showed nothing but forest for about twenty miles until the village of Marinopol on the other side. It was an ideal route for a lazy stroll through the woods.

The following morning after a final breakfast in Mega Burger which despite the staff's open contempt for me I had to admit served the best burgers I had ever eaten, I headed to Gomel bus station in search of a ride to Korma. The sun was out and it seemed as though summer was finally going to begin. It had to. I had passed fields on the train journey from Bobruisk that were full of cut wheat which lay rotting under the endless rains. For a rural economy such as Belarus' a wet summer could prove a financial disaster.

Buses to Korma were few and far between, situated as it was at the dead-end of a road that passed through nowhere significant and lying deep within the Zone. I passed time in the station cafe waiting for the afternoon service to depart with vagabonds who entered to buy cheap cups of coffee with coins begged on the station platform. Gypsy children with dirty faces entered and scrounged kopeks at tables before the exasperated manageress chased them out in a never ending game of catch-me-if-you-can. Eventually the bus pulled in and a handful of provincial travellers boarded for the journey north.

Along the way people disembarked at lonely bus shelters on the edge of wooden villages bearing Soviet names: Bolshevik, Kalinin, October, whilst all the while, out there to the east, looming on the horizon, the ever present shadow of the forest that had accompanied my journey through the country at every mile.

The passenger sitting beside me asked me where I was heading. A smartly dressed young man, he worked as a surgeon at Gomel hospital for which he was paid five hundred dollars a month. Many of his colleagues had emigrated abroad finding work in Europe and America where wages and living standards were far higher. Was he not tempted to leave too I asked.

'I have a wife and young son and I don't want him to grow up speaking German like my friend's children,' he replied, barely containing his disgust at the prospect of having Teutonic offspring.

'Better to stay, my grandparents are here and despite the difficulties it's my country. I shall not leave just because I can make money abroad.'

He disembarked at a bus stop far from anywhere and walked off along a muddied track towards a cluster of squat concrete buildings in the distance where his wife and child were no doubt waiting for him.

We continued north until the bus eventually pulled into the deserted bus station yard in the lonely outpost of Korma. By then I was the only passenger remaining on board, all the others having left long before. The sun of the morning had by now disappeared behind ominous black clouds that had appeared overhead and the sky crackled with the static of an impending storm. Walking past the town's hotel I briefly considered stopping for the night and sitting the weather out but my determination to keep moving pushed the thought aside.

'I'll find a cottage in the forest in which to spend the night,' I told myself, and with naive enthusiasm set off towards the river and the start of my journey through the woods.

TWENTY-TWO

Without knowing what lay ahead I followed the narrow road eastwards out of town with the sound of thunder rumbling from somewhere over the horizon ahead. Soon the small tangle of Korma's grey pre-fabricated apartment buildings came to an abrupt end and a hundred metres beyond that I passed the last of the town's wooden cottages that had somehow survived the Sovietisation of the town, almost immediately finding myself surrounded by wheat fields that spread out all around me. Nothing man-made was visible in the distance ahead, just the palisade of trees that spread out from north to south for as far as the eye could see. A wall of green that from where I stood looked impregnable and somewhat intimidating.

A farm worker returning from a day in the fields pushed her bicycle slowly up the sloping road towards me. Keen to confirm what had been marked on my map I asked her what exactly lay ahead of me.

'Nothing but the villages of Klyapin and klyapinskaya Buda, and beyond that nothing but forest.'

For once my map had been right.

'Be careful of the wolves in the forest,' she added seriously when I told her that I planned to cross that forest, before she continued wheeling her bicycle onwards towards the town.

A half hour later I arrived at an old pontoon constructed of rusting plates of steel that spanned the narrow river. A fisherman stood leaning on a handrail smoking a cigarette.

'Where are you going young man?' he asked as I passed him.

'The last village.'

'You'll not make it by nightfall and there's a storm coming,' he said, prodding his chin at the dark clouds that hung ominously over the forests I was about to enter.

'I'd sit it out if I were you or wait for a car, the forest is no place to be at night especially in a storm.'

But despite the ominous black clouds in the distance I enjoyed the feeling of moving forward, not knowing quite what lay ahead of me. It was ultimately the answer to the question I was repeatedly asked on my journey through the region: Why was I here?

On a subconscious level I suppose it was in part to re-connect with the primeval feeling of discovery which us Westerners with our work days spent in cubicles and weekends spent grazing in air-conditioned shopping centres have somehow

148

managed to suppress. And Belarus whilst being in the geographical heart of Europe was nonetheless an unknown corner of the Continent, a void on the map over which not long before was written 'Beware, here be dragons.' I was here to slay my dragon.

Ignoring the fisherman's counsel I continued across the rusting pontoon before stepping onto the gravel track that would eventually lead me to the two distant villages hidden somewhere in the forest. Old radiation signs erected long ago, the paint on them long since worn off by the passing of time, greeted my arrival on the eastern bank, forbidding me to leave the track and enter the forest. I walked on surrounded on both sides by marshland and beautifully coloured fields that were once a part of the collective farm but were now too contaminated to be turned by the plough, filled instead with wild flowers over which darted swallows and butterflies. Breathing in the fresh air I felt an intense sense of contentment to be alone in nature. And then the rain started.

Gently at first, just small drops that made little circles as they hit the gravelly track, but as I continued to walk on, the track leaving the open marshland behind and instead forging its way into the forest, the rain grew steadily fiercer as though sent as a reminder that I had no right entering this burnt edge of Belarus. Distant thunder rumbled closer and lightning lit the grey sky as the rains quickly turned into a vicious downpour that immediately turned the track to a river of mud and grit that flowed over my Converse, soaking my feet. Deciding on the lesser of two evils I ignored the radiation signs and left the road seeking shelter under the forest canopy instead. I had left most of my belongings in Gomel, deciding instead to carry as little as possible for the walk meaning I had neither a tent nor waterproof jacket, foolishly not having considered the possibility of such inclement weather. All I did have in my small rucksack was a groundsheet, some socks and t-shirts. The trees however provided no real shelter from the storm and so with no other choice and not wanting to return to the pontoon and an inevitable 'I told you so' look from the fisherman, I returned to the track, walking on in the hope of quickly finding somewhere dry in which to sit out the rain.

The prospect of a warm cottage in the forest where I might spend the night pushed me on in the face of the rains but after another couple of miles, cold, wet, and with no sign of any houses I started to contemplate the very real possibility of having to spend the night out in the open. Just then in the distance I heard the rumbling of a vehicle racing along the track. I stuck my arm out hoping to be seen and for pity to be taken on me as a truck appeared over the brow of the hill. However the driver who was ensconced high up in the warmth of the cabin ignored my appeal for help and hurtled by without slowing, soaking me in muddy water. There had been occasions on my drive through the countryside where I had not stopped to pick up hitchhiking mushroom pickers having not been in the mood for company. This was my payback.

On I trudged for another hour soaked to the skin, my eyes constantly scanning the woods in search of some kind of abandoned building in which to take shelter but there was nothing except trees for as far as my eyes could penetrate. Eventually I came to a rusting signpost that indicated there was a village some two kilometres further along the road. My body instantly warmed at the prospect of sitting in front of a log fire whilst a kindly babushka prepared a warm meal for me. On I walked, oblivious to the rains, whistling a happy tune and inwardly laughing at the fisherman's concerned warning until I reached the turn off and my heart sank. There was nothing left of the village except a wooden cross. I wiped the rain water from the brass inscription plate. It read: Village founded 1543. Abandoned 1991. Buried 2008.

There was perhaps another six or seven miles of walking to do until I made it to the first village and by then it would be midnight, a time when people would be reluctant to open their doors to an unexpected knock. But then, just as I started to prepare myself mentally for a miserable night spent sleeping in the woods, I heard a noise approaching from the stormy darkness behind me and soon after I was illuminated by the yellow light of car headlights. The vehicle passed by at speed ignoring my sodden wave, but then slowed, no doubt the occupants deciding whether to pick up a stranger in the forest at night, before eventually stopping. The steamy passenger window of an old Volga sedan rolled down to reveal a family of seven crammed into the car.

'Get in,' the driver said, cutting me off as I began to explain where I was heading.

I removed my backpack and squeezed onto the back seat next to four young children and a beautiful young woman in a velour tracksuit.

'Where are you heading?' the driver's wife in the front passenger seat asked, as we sped on through the woods.

'But there's nothing after Klyapinskaya Buda except forest,' she said, confused by my answer.

'You can't be in the forest alone at night,' the young woman beside me said, leaning as far away from me as possible, trying to avoid getting her tracksuit wet.

'Nobody ever goes into the forest at night.'

We drove on at speed, splashing through giant puddles that had filled the dips in the track, banging our heads on the ceiling of the car as we hit submerged potholes, until after sometime the headlights of the car illuminated a handful of miserable looking buildings in an abandoned settlement on the edge of the forest. Consisting of little more than two boarded up two-storied apartment buildings and a concrete bus shelter, it was as bleak an outpost as I'd seen on my journey in the Zone, and yet for some inexplicable reason I can't explain I suddenly told the driver to stop the car and let me out. Perhaps I thought that if the family would see the derelict buildings I would be forced to spend the night in they would take pity on me and offer a warm bed in their home, maybe tracksuit girl would let me share hers. But as I climbed out of the warmth of the car, hoping someone would stop me and tell me how stupid I was being by risking hypothermia or a mauling by a wolf, nobody said a word, as though spending a night in an abandoned Soviet bus shelter during a thunder storm was considered a perfectly reasonable thing to do in the provinces of Belarus. I looked at tracksuit girl with a look that I hoped she would read as: 'Invite me to stay and who knows where the future may lead, we might fall in love and move to Gomel together. I could buy you as many tracksuits as you want.' But she wasn't a mind reader. That or she just didn't need any more velour in her life.

'Well I guess I'll just spend the night here then...,' I said, slowly closing the door as the rain lashed down on me, waiting, hoping, for someone, anyone, to stop me.

'OK, good luck,' the driver said cheerily, and with that tracksuit girl pulled the door closed without a second glance and the car accelerated off along the track. My last chance of a warm bed disappeared into the darkness.

I ran over to the bus shelter, which was no more than a small concrete shed with a wooden plank inside it balanced on bricks, and sat there staring out into the rain filled darkness that enveloped the hamlet. The only sounds were that of water running off the roofs of the abandoned buildings and the thunder that was slowly growing louder with every deep rumble. I changed my t-shirt and socks and sat on the wooden bench of the shelter protected from the worst of the rains.

And there I sat eating a chocolate bar in the dark as the storm intensified and the trees swayed in the howling wind as though I was on the set of some Scandinavian film noire movie, but despite the storm and the thunder I must have eventually nodded off to sleep because I woke some hours later in the dead of night, upright and shivering whilst the rain lashed into the bus shelter at a vicious angle. I needed to find somewhere dry to take shelter in but although I knew that the village of Klyapin and tracksuit girl must be somewhere nearby I had no idea how far along the track it was and I wasn't keen on getting caught out on the road in the middle of the storm again. Instead, using the light from my phone, I ran over to one of the abandoned apartment buildings, threw my bag over a ground floor balcony and heaved myself up. The door of the apartment was loosely boarded with planks which I leveraged off before entering into the darkness of what was probably once someone's living room. It was empty but fortunately was dry. I found a spot in the furthest corner and sat there waiting for morning to come.

TWENTY-THREE

The silence of a provincial dawn was broken by the crow of cockerels coming from somewhere behind a row of trees. The village of Klyapin and a warm bed had unbeknownst to me been situated just a few hundred metres away around a bend in the track. Cold and hungry and with angry skies above I left the derelict building and began walking back along the track in wet shoes towards Korma. Torn branches and forest debris thrown around by the storm littered the way. After a few miles I heard a machine approaching and soon a small tractor appeared along the road attached to the back of which was a small cart containing three crouching babushkas who were sheltering from the rain under black umbrellas. I climbed in with them and slowly chugged back along the track to Korma.

I spent the day drifting in and out of sleep under the warm blankets of the town's hotel. My waking hours were divided between watching Soviet war films on the television set in the lobby and scanning the ominously dark skies, hoping for signs that the rainstorm would eventually blow itself out. It seemed however as though it would continue forever. The empty main square on which the hotel stood had turned into a lake of brown water in which were reflected the town's administrative buildings above which the national flag fluttered in the breeze. The only sign that there was in fact any kind of life out there beyond the hotel was the town's policeman who drove his patrol car around the town in slow circles, appearing in the flooded square in front of the hotel like clockwork every ten minutes.

In the evening I left the warmth of the hotel in search of food, stumbling upon a run-down restaurant on the edge of town owned by an Armenian immigrant. We sat together in the empty dining room sharing a bottle of Ararat cognac whilst he poured out his frustrations at running a business in provincial Belarus.

'There's simply no money here, so I usually only open the kitchen on weekends. I would be better off getting a job on the farm I suppose, a steady wage at least, but I borrowed money from the bank to open this place, so I have no choice but to carry on,' he said despondently.

I returned to the hotel in the relentless rain, skidding along liquid back paths that passed by dimly lit apartments. People stood on their balconies smoking in silence, blowing fumes into the blackness of a provincial night. The only other guest in the hotel, a Moldovan businessman in town to buy farm machinery from the collective farm, was relaxing on the lobby sofa in his vest that stretched tightly around his rotund torso, flirting with the buxom receptionist. I returned to my room, chased a sleeping tablet down with a beer and after some time fell asleep to the muffled sound of a familiar female voice coming from Moldovan's room next door.

TWENTY-FOUR

S unlight flooded into the room through the transparent curtains, warming the side of my face and waking me from a deep sleep. The storm had finally passed over the region revealing a vast sky that was once again azure and cloudless. I left my key at the empty reception desk and in clothes that smelt horribly of dampness bought two bottles of vodka in a corrugated shop and re-traced my footsteps along the muddy footpaths out of Korma and back towards the pontoon that spanned the river. A car heading in the same direction stopped and offered me a ride. Yuri was on his way to catch fish that his wife would later prepare for supper. I asked him about the wolves that inhabited the woods I would be walking through.

'Don't worry about the wolves they won't harm you. It's the bears you need to be careful of,' he said with a malicious grin.

I crossed the fast flowing Sozh with the heat rising, the dampness in my clothes and the squelching in my shoes evaporating with every step. It felt good to feel the warmth of the

159

sun on my face again after so long spent under cold grey skies. After a couple of miles I heard a car approaching and stuck my hand out.

Valentina was heading to the village of Klyapin to collect her mother who needed hospital treatment in town.

'You must be crazy, did nobody tell you that it's dangerous to go walking alone in the forest?' she said when I told her of my night in the abandoned hamlet.

'Why didn't you go to Nesvizh like most tourists?'

She asked about my journey through the region.

'Well it's good you speak Russian or who knows what would have happened to you. You're a foreigner and people don't have much here in the Zone. Desperate people can do desperate things.'

Wolves, bears, people...the only thing nobody mentioned was the one real danger that was all around us. I asked how she felt raising kids in a town situated in the most radiated part of the country.

'Of course I don't like it, you think I want to raise my children here in the Zone or feed them contaminated food from the forest? No. I wish I was able to feed them fresh seafood and vegetables like you no doubt eat in England but I don't have that choice. I have two university degrees and yet I make just $300 a month, so tell me how exactly can I change something?'

She said all this with a complete lack of bitterness in her voice. In fact, in all my time in the countryside, despite the hardships, despite the low wages and small pensions, despite living in contaminated lands, the people never sought sympathy, never showed anger, never wanted pity. The way the locals continued to laugh and smile through it all was testament to the strength of character of the Belarusian people.

Valentina dropped me off at the entrance to the village of Klyapin which now contained no more than twenty pretty cottages and a village shop that had closed down years ago judging by the empty shelves inside. At the far edge of the village the footpath split in two directions. I called over the picket fence of a cottage and after a few minutes the owner appeared from his garden clutching a watering can. I asked him the way to Klyapinskaya Buda which was the last village.

'My son will be happy show you,' he said before calling out his name.

A young man with an intelligent face appeared from the house surprised to find a foreigner in his village.

'Follow the left-hand path to the school and wait for me there, I need to finish some work first but I won't be long,' he said.

The path headed behind the cottages and led to a pretty school building set in a well tended garden. I entered the gate and walked the empty corridors passing tidy classrooms containing empty desks and children's cots before stumbling upon the headmistress who was on her hands and knees scrubbing the hallway.

'The children will be arriving tomorrow for a summer-camp so we are getting everything ready for their arrival,' she said whilst wringing out a dirty rag into a metal pail.

It seemed an odd choice of place to send kids for the summer located as it was in the middle of a radiated forest.

'Well the government declared the village clean from contamination not long ago so they get sent here now,' she said. 'Better for them to be here than in the city anyway.'

She invited me to drink tea in her brightly painted classroom. It was clear that the teachers had invested their energy into the school to make it as pleasant as possible for the students, but despite the village having recently been declared safe there was bad news from the local administration in Korma.

'They plan to close the school next year, we only have seven children now from the two villages so it doesn't make sense to keep it open. I have no idea what will happen to us,' she said sadly.

The school was the only employer in Klyapin and Klyapinskaya Buda and besides the teachers, the school employed a gardener, maintenance man, cleaner and cook. If the school closed they'd all be out of a job and facing uncertain futures.

'The farm closed years ago so there is nowhere else to find work in the villages. I don't know what we will do without the school, but we'll survive, we've survived worse.'

Afterwards I sat on a bench waiting for my guide to come and show me the path. The school's handyman joined me on the porch for a smoke. He wore a t-shirt across which was written 'Fuck me I'm Irish'. In a region where many people could only afford to buy clothes at second hand shops that sold cheap imported items you were always sure to find people wearing random slogans, the meaning of which the wearers no doubt did not understand. I'd once seen an elderly man in Minsk wearing a t-shirt across which was written 'Big Dave's Berlin Stag Do'. I presumed the old man had never actually met big Dave or been on his stag do.

'The headmistress told me the region has been declared safe from radiation now. That must be a relief to the villagers,' I said.

He laughed cynically.

'You know why they did that right? People living in contaminated regions receive bonus pay from the government each month, so now Batska is declaring the whole country safe in order to stop the handouts. When the politicians are building dachas down here I'll believe it's safe.'

The young man with the intelligent face appeared at the school and we left, following a path that passed the abandoned farm buildings and cow sheds of what was once the collective farm.

'When I was young there were houses there, and there, and over there,' he said, pointing at what were now empty patches of discoloured grass.

I had friends in all the houses and after school we'd explore and ride our bikes around but most families left as soon as they were offered re-locations. My parents worked at the school, so we had to stay. I struggled for a long time with that and in truth I was angry at my parents for not leaving, but now as an adult I understand the sacrifice they made by staying behind.'

We walked on in the rising heat following the grassy path along the edge of the woods until after half an hour we reached a gravel track that led towards the village of Klyapinskaya Buda.

'Thank you for making this journey,' he said as we shook hands preparing to part ways.

'Young Belarusian people have no real interest in the provinces. My friends in Minsk have no idea where Korma is on the map and there is little interest in the traditions of the villages so you coming here and writing a book about the region is important. Maybe foreigners will read it and want to come in the future,' he added finally, smiling at the thought.

The narrow road meandered for an hour through native woodland until as the sun passed overhead I finally reached the end of the track at the pretty village of Klyapinskaya Buda. Beyond the village there would be nothing but trackless forest for mile after mile.

I knocked on the door of a ramshackle cottage to ask directions through the woods, disturbing a shirtless man who stumbled out into the bright afternoon light with bloodshot eyes. Not understanding what it was I was asking, either due to my accent or his intoxication, he waved me away obviously annoyed by my disturbing him, slamming the wooden door of his house shut with a bang. I continued along the path towards the centre of the hamlet where I found an elderly man unloading cut grass from a cart outside his cottage with a huge pitchfork. He invited me into his garden to drink fruit juice he'd made with forest berries. Was there a path through the woods to the village of Marinopol I asked as we slaked our thirst in the afternoon heat. Despite there being nothing marked on the map, there had to be some contact between the villages on either side of the forest, if not now then in the past.

Speaking a provincial mixture of Russian and Belarusian that I found hard to follow he explained that there was indeed a track of sorts that mushroom pickers had used in the past but which ended at the swamp. Beyond that he don't know. It was the first I had heard of the swamp.

'I was born here but I've never been to Marinopol and nobody has come here from the other side of the forest for as long as I can remember. Why would they, we don't have anything here that they need.'

I'd noticed that often in the countryside, people were usually unaware of life beyond the boundaries of their village. There was always chores to do, gardens to tend, vegetables and juices to prepare for the long winter months. Lazy strolls through the woods were not something people had the time for. Those were the preserve of people who had aimless lives with nothing important to do. People like me.

The old man went into his house, returning soon after clutching a large bottle of fruit juice in his hands which he insisted on handing me before leading me to the edge of the fields that ran along the back of the village and pointing me in the direction of a small path that headed into the forest. I shook his bony hand and set off, following the sandy track through the stubby wheat field until I came to the point where the trees began. I turned, looking back for a final glimpse of civilisation like a mariner not knowing when he would see land again. The old man, satisfied that I was heading in the right direction, turned back towards his cottage. I was alone.

TWENTY-FIVE

The track that led into the woods was well trodden and easy to follow at first, compacted as it was by the feet of the few local foragers reckless enough to seek their meals from the contaminated forest floor. I followed the meandering path deeper and deeper into the twilight keen to make steady progress. With about twenty miles of walking in front of me I would have to get a move on in order to get through and reach the little hamlet of Marinopol before nightfall.

I continued on with confidence and excitement, however after an hour the path I'd been following suddenly disappeared beneath my feet, forcing me to search for it among the trees before eventually finding it again somewhere further on in the distance where it rose out of a bed of pine needles. Occasionally I'd see animal tracks criss-crossing the compacted mud of the path and I crossed my fingers that they belonged to nothing larger than a hedgehog or a squirrel. A violent squirrel was something I felt I could kick the shit out of without too much trouble should the need arise. But the further I walked, the denser

167

the woods and undergrowth became forcing me at times to scramble through dense bushes and climb over fallen tree trunks which lay across the path.

These were forests untouched by the saws and axes of men ever since the disaster, covered as they were by deadly radioactive particles, but I didn't want to think about that, instead I continued chalking off the miles, the path steadily becoming harder to follow, disappearing for ever increasing stretches, people no doubt rarely came this far into the depths. However just when the path would melt into the debris and I wasn't sure in which direction to head I'd see an old discarded vodka bottle on the forest floor and I knew I must be heading in a direction once taken by others. This was the first time in my life that I could remember ever being truly alone in nature, miles from anywhere or anyone. At first every unfamiliar noise, every snap of a branch or squawk of a bird caused my adrenalin levels to spike as I scanned the woods for a wolf or maniac, but soon I relaxed, no longer even bothering to turn and look when I heard an unfamiliar sound.

Throughout history Belarusians have sought shelter in the forests when invaders came to their land, hiding there until the threat had passed. It was in these very forests that partisan units resisted the invading German troops. From the woods they would appear, striking suddenly at railway lines and infrastructure before melting back into the darkness from where they came. Ghosts of the forests. Across the country partisans would appear to harass and kill the occupiers and their collaborators. Jews, communists, Christians, all hiding together, waiting to avenge what had been done to their families and land.

On I walked in an easterly direction through the dappled light of the forest canopy for a couple more hours lost in my thoughts as with time the forest floor changed consistency, becoming spongy and damper under foot, the path often turning completely to mud, huge puddles of it in which I would at times sink ankle deep forcing me to search for a dry route around the bogs. The sun's rays were now no longer lighting the forest floor from above, the dusk of early evening slowly filling the wood making it hard for me to be certain I was following any kind of path at all at times as my eyes adjusted to the failing light, however as long as I continued east it would be impossible to get truly lost, eventually I would hit a road, even if it took a couple of days. I continued on until quite suddenly, deep inside the radiated forest and far from anywhere, I took a step and sank calf deep into squelching mud. I had reached the swamp.

I explored along the edge in each direction, searching for a dry way around the water but eventually gave up. Stretching for what seemed like miles, it was simply too big to avoid. I weighed up my options. It was already getting dark in the forest meaning I could make it out into the middle of the swamp but then be enveloped in the blackness of the night not knowing which way to continue, an unappealing prospect. And so with little choice I spread my sleeping sheet on the ground and decided to wait for the morning.

It wasn't something I had wanted to do. So far I had not been too concerned by the radiation doses I had been taking on my trip. I'd spent my journey amongst local people who had spent decades surrounded by the invisible danger, allowing me to console myself, perhaps naively, that there was in reality little to fear from a few weeks spent in the contaminated region. But here, deep in the forest and all alone, I felt vulnerable for the first time. Every step I took, every branch I touched, I imagined was disturbing particles of radiation that would seep into my skin. Every time I took a breath I imagined the radiation my lungs and blood stream were consuming and the mutations within that were slowly beginning to form. But there was no point dwelling on it after all I was here by my own choice. Instead, I laid out my plastic sheet and drank the last of the fruit juice the old man had given me, and despite the insects that crawled on me and the thoughts of wolves and radiation, I eventually fell asleep in the eerie silence of the world's most radiated forest.

TWENTY-SIX

The sound of birdsong filled the woods at dawn as dappled light filtered through the tops of the trees lighting my mud covered legs and feet. There was a refreshing chill in the morning air and marsh-haze rose ghost-like over the water on the swamp. I'd had a night of vivid dreams, which was becoming the norm on my trip, in which I had been chased by a pack of wolves with glowing eyes through a forest. After stretching the aches from a night on the hard floor from my body I waited for the sun to rise and warm the water a little before stripping, wrapping my backpack in my groundsheet and entering the opaqueness of the swamp.

Slowly I waded into the thick soupy water, my legs sinking into the mud, parting bullrushes and prickly reeds that clung to my exposed body as I passed through them, forging a way slowly onwards. My feet followed the muddy bottom down until the water reached my waist forcing me to lift my belongings above my head and wade on as the occasional bird, startled by my unexpected presence, took flight from the reeds, squawking as it frantically flapped its wings into the air. I used the rotting branches of dead trees to pull me along through the liquid that was becoming thicker and increasingly choked with plant life with every laboured step. Sometimes a leg would sink deep into the muddy depths, and I was unable to free it without using my hand to leverage it out meaning that after an hour I had travelled no more than fifty metres. I lay my bag on a dry patch of plants and rested, the sweat of exertion mixing with the swamp mud on my face and running into my eyes, blinding me. But I continued slowly ploughing forwards, not sure how much further there was to go, cringing every time something brushed against my legs in the depths of the swamp until just when I started to wonder if I'd ever get across to dry land, the bullrushes parted and a thick line of trees appeared across the water about a hundred metres in the distance giving me renewed strength to continue.

I waded on slowly until I saw an old fence post rising like Excalibur out of the water, and then another and another, no doubt the rotting boundary of what had once upon a time been the collective farm. My legs carried me forwards for another hour in slow heaving steps that made sucking noises as I lifted my legs from the muddy bottom until with time the water gradually became shallower and the bulrushes sparser. Soon it was below my waist and then below my knees and eventually I could see my muddied feet beneath me, cut and bleeding from the sharp reeds I had trampled beneath me.

Exhausted and thirsty from the endeavour I lay on the first piece of dry land I came to amongst the line of trees, eating the last of my chocolate supplies before following the rotting fence posts that stood lopsided in a ramshackle line through the forest. I kept them in sight, confident that they must lead to a settlement of some kind and after some time shapes began appearing in the trees ahead. I walked on finding old wooden crosses that stood leaning at fallen angles where they had been placed perhaps a hundred years before. I passed through the old graveyard before finding the remnants of a path that led past wooden cottages that had long been abandoned and were now being devoured by the forest, floorboards and earth becoming one again. Trees grew through living rooms and kitchens floors, slowly tearing the empty houses apart.

I left the abandoned village following a path that ran along the edge of the woods and then out into the open, shadowing overgrown fields that had not been turned by the farmer's plough in decades. On top of an old telegraph pole rested a huge crane's nest long abandoned by its builders, without the farmers to scythe the fields the cranes would not return to hunt each year. And then at midday with the bright sun above me I rounded a corner on the path and suddenly found myself standing in front of three pretty wooden cottages. The hamlet of Marinopol. I had made it through the forest.

TWENTY-SEVEN

I knocked on the doors of the cottages in search of something to quench my thirst having not drunk since finishing the fruit juice the previous evening but there was no response at any of the houses. Instead I filled a bucket at the village well and doused myself in the cool water, washing the mud and smell of the swamp from my body, but I thought better than to drink it. The radiation particles that settled over the region thirty years ago had long penetrated the soil, contaminating the region's ground water. Instead I took a shot of vodka from one of the bottles I had carried with me from Korma. I really was becoming a true Belarusian.

With no response at the houses I left the village following a narrow dusty road through fields of wild flowers that were dotted with farm buildings which had been stripped of anything of value and abandoned long ago. Ravens watched me pass by slowly, perched on wooden telegraph poles that had long since lost their wires. I must have walked for an hour in the heat of the summer's day until passing a rusting sign which pointed me on to the village of Gorky. With the sun burning from above my pace became steadily slower, my feet hurting more with every step taken on the stony road until eventually after passing more broken cattle sheds I entered the old logging village.

In search of some inhabitants I walked the rutted main street of the village but it was as abandoned as the broken farms buildings that had shadowed my journey from Marinopol. The only house still standing upright had its doors and windows boarded up with planks. A handwritten sign had been nailed to the fence: 'Please do not break in, we have nothing inside worth taking.' The old bus stop stood on the main road through the village half hidden by weeds and nettles, waiting for services that had long stopped running to this forgotten corner of the country. Everything else had been bulldozed and buried.

I rested in the shade of willow trees on a small concrete bridge that spanned a small tributary of the river Pokats, removing my shoes to let my feet recover from the walk, but with my thirst unquenched and desperate for water I had no choice but to continue.

In the silence of the evacuated Belarusian countryside I trudged on, slowly heading towards the village of Soboli that my map indicated was located a few miles further down the road, the thought of a cold drink keeping me going despite my exhaustion. The journey had destroyed my running shoes with gaping holes having been worn into the rubber bottoms meaning that the only thing standing between the soles of my feet and the sharp stones of the road were my socks. Dust and grit entered the cuts on my blistered soles adding to my discomfort, however, exhausted and thirsty, I eventually arrived at the entrance to the village of Soboli after an hour.

The outskirts consisted of the usual collection of rotting barns and the demolished brick sheds of the old collective farm and I walked on searching for signs of life not wanting to entertain the thought that Soboli might be just another abandoned outpost of the Zone. But then as I walked along the back of the village, passing empty cottages and slowly losing hope, I saw crisp white bed linen hanging out to dry on a line in a well tended garden. I turned down a grassy path that ran alongside the house, and there on a bench next to an abandoned concrete shop in the middle of the wooden village, sat two elderly men dressed in their Sunday best.

TWENTY-EIGHT

O ne of the men went to the well and lowered the bucket into the water below, the refreshing echo of its splash rose up and echoed around the silent settlement. Too thirsty to care about the possible contamination any more I gulped down the clear cool water, finally slaking my thirst.

More elderly men appeared from their wooden cottages no doubt having heard the unexpected bubble of conversation that punctured the silence of village life, gathering around and asking where I'd come from. And when I told them they looked at me confused. Nobody ever came from the other side, not since the disaster they said. How did I manage to cross the swamp one asked. And when I told them they asked how life was over there on the other side, if the farms had been closed down there as they had in their village. One elderly man dressed in the smart threadbare clothes of the proud but poor went to his cottage, returning soon after clutching a hunk of black bread and a large slice of greasy pig fat. I answered their questions between bites and then took my muddied backpack and placed it on the wooden table around which the villagers sat, proceeding to pull out one of the bottles of vodka I had carried with me through the forest from Korma. The old men all said ooh in unison. And then I pulled out the other bottle and they all said aah, rubbing their hands as expectant smiles spread across their faces. One villager went and opened a blue postbox nailed to the wooden fence of what had once been the post office, it contained two chipped glasses yellowed with age. I opened the bottles and poured the liquid into the glasses, and we took it in turns to drink the clear liquid down. Finally, my feet stopped hurting.

We continued to sit on the bench next to the abandoned shop in Soboli making toasts and answering as best I could the villagers questions about the outside world: Would there be war between Russia and America? Did pensioners have enough to eat in England? And when the vodka was finished one of the men went to his cottage and returned with an old plastic bottle containing a murky liquid. The villagers smiled and rubbed their hands as he poured moonshine into my glass, asking me to try his home-made brew. And the eldest man in the group, a man who lived in a pretty cottage with a red star nailed above the door which indicated a war hero lived there said, 'We shall remember this day until the end.'

'That won't be long Nikolai Nikolaevich,' someone replied.

And we drank the moonshine until my head span and my eyelids became heavy. And Nikolai Nikolaevich noticing my tiredness invited me to go with him. And I followed him to his cottage which was shaded by a huge oak tree that in its long life had witnessed the sad history of Belarus, the invasions, the radiation and evacuations. We entered a back door that led to an unexpectedly bright tidy kitchen where his wife, a pretty grey haired babushka with a warm smile stood preparing soup on the stove.

'My English friend is tired,' he said to her. 'Let him lie down for a while Luda.'

'Come with me young man,' she said, leading me through a living room decorated with black and white photos of village life from past times when the shop was not abandoned and there was work to be had for all. Luda pulled aside a lace curtain that led onto a bright bedroom containing a metal bedstead painted in Belarusian-blue like everything else in the provinces.

'Rest here, it's the most comfortable bed in the village,' she said, fluffing the pillows for me.

I sat on the edge of the bed too exhausted to undress myself as Luda pulled my t-shirt over my head and helped me out of my muddy socks, insisting on taking them to wash.

And finally I lay down on the soft bed, my head resting on a cotton pillow case decorated with native village patterns, and there in the pretty bedroom watched over by an array of wooden icons in the corner of the room I fell into a sleep deeper than any I had had on my journey through the country.

And that night on the blue bedstead in the wooden village of Soboli I dreamt a vivid dream. There was a beautiful girl with long flowing hair in which she wore a colourful garland of flowers. And she wore a white dress that was decorated with the same native patterns as the pillow on which my head lay. And she asked me what I saw on my trip through the land and I said, 'Let me show you.' And we flew up into the azure sky over the radiated forest and I showed her the swamp and the forests I had crossed, the people I had met, the places I had seen. And after I had shown her it all she turned to me with beautiful grey eyes and said, 'You are ours now. You are ours.'

ACKNOWLEDGEMENTS

Although I made my journey alone, the book would not have turned out as I had wanted without having someone to bounce ideas off and offer encouragement. For this I turned to my girlfriend Alina who I knew I could rely upon for some brutal Belarusian honesty where it was needed. Thank you.

Thanks to my mother who taught me the difference between stalk and stork.

Also, thanks to KR and YG for their support.

AUTHOR BIO

This is Mr. Bald's first book but he enjoyed writing it so much that one day he will write another. In the meantime you can enjoy his YouTube channel: bald and bankrupt.

Made in United States
North Haven, CT
13 March 2023

33994549R00121